*the*
# Vegan
# Pantry

# the Vegan Pantry

### 60 naturally delicious recipes
### for modern vegan food

## Dunja Gulin
### photography by William Reavell

LONDON · NEW YORK

**Senior Designer** Iona Hoyle

**Commissioning Editor** Céline Hughes

**Editor** Nathan Joyce

**Head of Production** Patricia Harrington

**Editorial Director** Julia Charles

**Art Director** Leslie Harrington

**Prop Stylist** Jo Harris

**Food Stylists** Emily Kydd & Rosie Reynolds

**Indexer** W. Stephen Gilbert

First published in the UK in 2014
by Ryland Peters & Small
20–21 Jockey's Fields
London WC1R 4BW
and
519 Broadway, 5th Floor
New York, NY 10012
www.rylandpeters.com

10 9 8 7 6 5 4 3 2 1

Text © Dunja Gulin 2014

Design and photographs
© Ryland Peters & Small 2014

ISBN: 978-1-84975-489-7

A CIP record for this book is available from the
British Library.

A CIP record for this book is available from the
Library of Congress

Printed in China

# contents

# introduction

It is important that you read this introduction. All of it! I'm aware that my cookbooks have introductions that are a bit longer than usual, but I really think that understanding the principles behind my recipes will make your cooking and the choice of ingredients much easier. You will also feel that you are not just following the recipes, but understanding the building blocks upon which you can create your own dishes, without the fear of messing up – the fear that haunts many beginners.

Firstly, I'd like to introduce myself and share with you my approach to cooking and my way of thinking about diets and lifestyles.

I started my health-food journey as a teenager, which led me to vegetarian, vegan and macrobiotic recipes that I tried and loved. During my academic studies I found time to attend natural-cooking training programmes, which were mostly on macrobiotic food. After graduating from university, my love of healthy cooking led me away from my vocation and towards my passion – combining different cooking styles and philosophies to create a way of healthy cooking and eating with one goal in mind – to eat the best that nature has to offer, based on individual approach and common sense. That is why this cookbook is really a fusion of different cooking styles (vegan, macrobiotic and raw) that I have incorporated into my daily routine over the years, and which, in my opinion, nicely complement each other and bring balance to my diet. Naturally, only entirely vegan recipes are included in this book. This doesn't mean you have to be a strict vegan to enjoy them, though!

Some people think that just by avoiding animal foods they will stay healthy. I have to say that I do not agree. There are a number of vegan foods – white bread, refined sugar, margarine and TSP (textured soy protein) – which can have a negative effect on health if consumed on a daily or even weekly basis in the long-term. So, there has to be criteria more complex than just that the food is vegan in order for a food to qualify as healthy. It also has to be as unprocessed as possible, because unprocessed foods are so much more nutritious.

You have to understand that the body is always trying to reach some kind of balance, so, for example, after a binge on meat, the body is asking for ice-cream! After a salty cheeseburger there has to be some sugary soda! However, eventually the body may get so exhausted with these alternating extremes that, eventually, serious health problems can begin to occur.

Then, what happens if you make the decision to exclude meat products from your diet, but keep eating heavily refined foods? Most probably, imbalance! What I'm trying to say is really simple: with your decision to be vegan you'll need to start questioning your other food choices, take certain supplements and exclude refined foods from your diet in order to stay healthy. Read more about my suggestions on how to do this in the following pages.

I hope you enjoy this wonderful journey, with me watching over your shoulder and giving you tips and tricks when something goes wrong, because:

*'No one who cooks, cooks alone. Even at her most solitary, a cook in the kitchen is surrounded by generations of cooks past, the advice and menus of cooks present, the wisdom of cookbook writers.'* (Laurie Colwin)

# starting from scratch

There's a great feeling of satisfaction when you know that the foods you use in your everyday cooking come directly from nature. Building up your body from pure, natural foods is the best investment you can make and brings health and happiness on many different levels to you and those around you.

## Getting organized

Maybe you know people that can whip up a feast in no time and make cooking seem like the easiest thing in the world? Well, the most well-kept secret of all skilled chefs and cooks is that good organization is crucial! Let your food soak, pressure-cook, sprout, etc. while you're showering, cleaning, ironing, reading or playing with your kids – since not all stages of cooking need constant attention! This way, cooking can be a process that doesn't feel like it takes up much of your time. The worst thing is getting home, being hungry and not having anything ready, as this will result in a visit to the bakery across the street or the inevitable ordering of a takeaway. So, always try to have some cooked grains or beans in the fridge, or protein like seitan, tofu or tempeh, all of which you can easily transform into quick and healthy meals by adding some fresh veggies, a little oil and by applying some heat. I always say to my students that planning skills are as equally important as cooking skills – if you plan well, half of the work is already done!

Even if your schedule is pretty full and you occasionally use some canned foods to quicken the cooking process, bear in mind that even the best quality, organic canned foods have lost a lot of vital energy and nutrients. A good way to help ensure that you are getting the right amount of nutrients as well as to reduce your daily cooking time is to pre-cook some foods when you have time, and use them as the base for preparing meals when you get home from work. Grains and legumes, if cooked on their own, will keep in the fridge for 2–4 days, so this gives you the possibility to plan ahead.

Cooking is like a jigsaw puzzle: each part of the cooking process is like a small piece, and with patience and experience you'll be able to produce beautiful and creative paintings on your plate that you'll be able to enjoy with all your senses!

# basics

## cooking grains

Whole grains are an essential part of a healthy diet and a great source of complex carbohydrates, fibre/fiber, vitamins and minerals. A vegan diet rich in refined grains cannot be defined as healthy, so, in case your pantry isn't already packed with whole grains, grab your reusable shopping bag, run to buy the whole grains on my list, and never look back!

As you can see from the table, some grains can be soaked or dry-roasted before cooking, but it's not essential. Soaking hard grains (brown rice, barley, spelt etc.) makes them easier to digest, as does cooking them in a pressure cooker. Dry-roasting results in a nutty flavour. Adding soft grains (millet, amaranth, quinoa, buckwheat etc.) to boiling water cooks them more evenly and reduces stickiness.

## cooking legumes

Legumes are a class of nutritious vegetables that include peas, lentils and beans. They are a great source of protein, minerals and fibre. Eating vegan means, among other things, that you've decided to stop eating meat, but you need to have some protein on your plate, and legumes are just that: full of protein and low in fat!

Cooking dried legumes from scratch requires following a couple of steps to make them softer and easier to digest (reducing the gas-factor). I use the shock method, which involves cooking the legumes in enough water to cover them, and then adding a little cold water when needed – this 'shocks' the skins and makes the seed softer. I always add a piece of kombu when cooking legumes (Japanese style), as well as a bay leaf (my grandma's style), both of which are supposed to aid the digestion of beans and lentils.

| TYPE OF GRAIN | GRAIN : WATER RATIO (CUPS)* | COOKING TIME/MINS | OPTIONAL PREPARATION, BEFORE COOKING |
|---|---|---|---|
| BROWN RICE | 1:2 (COLD WATER) | 40–50 | SOAKING FOR 8 HOURS IN MEASURED AMOUNT OF WATER |
| WHITE RICE | 1:2 (BOILING WATER) | 20 | – |
| QUINOA | 1:2½ (BOILING WATER) | 15–20 | – |
| SPELT & BARLEY | 1:2 (COLD WATER) | 40–50 | SOAKING |
| AMARANTH | 1:3 (BOILING WATER) | 25 | – |
| BUCKWHEAT | 1:2 (BOILING WATER) | 15–20 | DRY-ROASTING |
| MILLET | 1:2 (BOILING WATER) | 15–20 | DRY-ROASTING |

\* 1 CUP = 240 ML (FOR LIQUID MEASURES). FOR DRY MEASURES, THE EQUIVALENT CUP WEIGHT IN GRAMS DEPENDS ON THE TYPE OF GRAIN. I FIND THAT MEASURING GRAINS AND WATER IN CUPS IS THE EASIEST AND QUICKEST WAY TO PREPARE THEM.

| TYPE OF LEGUME | SOAKING | COOKING TIME/MINS | TYPE OF POT |
|---|---|---|---|
| LENTILS (BROWN, GREEN, BELUGA, PUY) | NO | 30–40 | NORMAL, SHOCK METHOD |
| LENTILS (RED, YELLOW) | NO | 20–25 | NORMAL |
| SOFT BEANS (AZUKI, MUNG) | OPTIONAL | 45–60 | NORMAL, SHOCK METHOD |
| HARD BEANS (KIDNEY, HARICOT/NAVY, CHICKPEAS, TURTLE, BUTTER/LIMA ETC.) | YES | 60+ | USE PRESSURE COOKER FOR BEST RESULT |

## stocking your vegan pantry

Have a quick look at the list of staples that follows. Are there a lot of foods that you are already eating? If yes, that is really a good sign! But you might also find some more unusual ingredients that you feel are too exotic and you will never be able to incorporate them into your diet. A long time ago I thought so too, but just stay open and be patient...you'll see how wonderful new foods can be. They're not only tasty, but also rich in some nutrients other 'ordinary' foods cannot give you. It would be a shame to reject them just because they aren't part of traditional Western cooking traditions.

## pantry staples

### grains & pasta

Brown rice, millet (and millet flakes), quinoa, polenta and rolled oats are the grains and grain products that I use most frequently in my daily cooking. However, you will most probably also find amaranth, spelt, barley, wild rice and buckwheat stored somewhere in the back shelves, and I use them occasionally – in soups, stews, crackers and salads, as you will see in this book. Different types of whole grain and gluten-free pasta are great pantry staples too, for quick weekday meals.

### dried beans

I love to have both soft and hard beans available in my pantry – soft beans like red, green, brown and beluga lentils and azuki beans can all be prepared faster without soaking, while kidney, haricot/navy, borlotti beans and chickpeas which take a bit longer to cook and need soaking. Beans are a very important part of my diet and they are packed with nutrients and rich in protein. I never use canned beans, but there's no harm in having a couple of cans of organic beans in your pantry, for emergencies.

### oils & vinegars

The oil I use most frequently in cooking and seasoning is definitely olive oil. I always have two types of olive oil on hand: cheaper, neutral oil for cooking and extra-virgin olive oil for use in salads or to sprinkle at the end of cooking. I'm lucky that my grandma still supplies me with her own high-quality Istrian olive oil, but if you have to buy yours please try to invest a bit more money, as good-quality olive oil transforms the simplest foods. Sunflower and coconut oil are especially good for deep-frying and baking, and flaxseed and toasted sesame oil for seasoning. As for vinegars, it's useful to have apple cider vinegar and brown rice vinegar for seasoning salads, in small quantities. I should also mention umeboshi plum vinegar, which I use more as a condiment than as a vinegar – its salty, sour and fruity flavour deepens the taste of creamy soups, stews and vegetable dishes, and I highly recommend it as a staple on your pantry shelf!

### salt

Unrefined sea salt is the type of salt I use most frequently, but unrefined rock salt is also a great source of trace minerals and can be used on a daily basis. Both coarse and fine unrefined salt is good to have on hand; coarse for adding while cooking, and fine for finishing dishes. Avoid using table salt, and salt with added iodine!

### nuts & seeds

There are so many kinds of nuts and seeds, and I love all of them! Almonds, hazelnuts and walnuts are local to my area so I use them more often, and save the exotic kinds (such as cashews and macadamia nuts) for special recipes, especially in baking. From the seeds list, I highly recommend using sunflower, pumpkin and unhulled sesame seeds almost daily, since they are so rich in vital minerals. Flaxseed and chia seeds are both beneficial for digestion and especially rich in Omega 3- and 6- fatty acids, and I often soak or grind them and add them to breakfast porridge, soups, salads or desserts.

### herbs & spices

You'll notice that my style of cooking includes a lot of Mediterranean herbs and spices, which is not surprising since I grew up on the Adriatic coast! Dried oregano, thyme, basil, bay leaves, ground turmeric, ground ginger, fennel seeds, chilli powder, sweet paprika, peppercorns and curry powder are on my favourites list, but I sometimes also use cumin, cayenne pepper, cloves and cardamom powder to enhance the flavour of a particular dish. Choose your favourites and experiment substituting my suggestions with your own mixtures of herbs and spices!

## dried goods

Apart from grains and beans, which are also dried, there are a couple of other dried foods that I use regularly and suggest you use them too! Dried foods are concentrated and therefore richer in taste and nutrients; some dried foods even have healing properties (like shiitake mushrooms, for example, which boost the immune system and lower blood pressure, among many health benefits). Dried fruits such as raisins, apricots, dates, prunes, etc. are all great to have on hand to nibble on or to use in desserts. Sundried tomatoes and sundried shiitake mushrooms are two dried delicacies I have to have in my cupboard, and I use them to make some dishes even more yummy and creative!

Among the more exotic vegetables are dried sea vegetables, or seaweed. They are completely neglected in most Western cooking-styles, but I urge you to include them in your everyday cooking. As a great source of minerals straight from nature, seaweed is cheaper than multi-mineral supplements, and much tastier too. I use kombu, arame, wakame, nori, hijiki and agar-agar, and since all types of dried seaweed have an almost infinite shelf life, you don't have to worry that they will go bad if you don't use them as often as I do!

## vegan baking & dessert essentials

It's a good idea to have the following flours at home: unbleached plain/all-purpose flour, wholemeal/whole wheat flour, millet flour, fine cornmeal and rye flour. To make your vegan baked goods rise, you will need aluminium-free baking powder and a little bicarbonate of soda/baking soda. For sweetness I suggest using

brown rice syrup and pure maple syrup, and only occasionally demerara/raw brown sugar and agave syrup. It's a good idea to have desiccated/shredded coconut, cocoa powder, dark/bittersweet vegan chocolate, cinnamon and bourbon vanilla powder in your pantry so you can quickly prepare a healthy vegan dessert and not reach for the unhealthy stuff that shops are full of!

## thickeners

Cornflour/cornstarch, kuzu and arrowroot powder can each be used to thicken soups, stews, goulashes and desserts in the same way – diluted in a little cold water and added towards the end of cooking time. Cornflour/cornstarch is the most frequently used of the three, while kuzu powder is the really healthy one (and priced accordingly). I try to limit the use of thickeners as much as I can, but sometimes a teaspoon makes a huge difference in consistency.

## food supplements

Whole foods and a versatile vegan diet will give you plenty of nutrients, and if you have a healthy lifestyle, without too much stress, you probably won't need to take any food supplements on a daily basis, except for vitamin B12, which you should take for three consecutive months per year. If you're eating cheese, fish or eggs from time to time then you don't have to worry about it so much, but checking your B12 levels every couple of years would be wise. Another problem that many vegans (and non-vegans as well for that matter) have to face is iron deficiency. If detailed blood tests reveal you have an iron deficiency, I suggest taking an organic liquid iron supplement free of alcohol, additives and preservatives. In case you're diagnosed with anaemia, make sure the cause is not low thyroid function before you start taking iron supplements.

## perishable staples

Here is a list of foods that might need to stay refrigerated or kept in a cool place, especially in the warmer months of the year, to avoid spoilage.

## vegetables

Stuff your fridge, pantry and cupboard with as many types of seasonal and organic veggies as you can! Root vegetables that grow deep in the soil are full of nutrients, providing us with strength and stability; they also add sweet, strong and rich flavours to our tables. Carrots, celeriac/celery root, parsnips and beet(root) are most commonly used but turnips and radishes are equally good for you. Sweet potatoes and potatoes are loved by many and cooking without onions and garlic is almost impossible to imagine, so always have them close to your chopping board! Round veggies like pumpkins and cabbages have great vital power and last for a long time, while gentle leafy greens such as chard, spinach, kale, lettuce, rocket/arugula, broccoli, mizuna, wild greens, etc. provide us with many important minerals and vitamins and should be eaten, either raw and cooked, with almost every meal! And this list isn't complete without the almighty fresh ginger, your best friend to help fight colds, flu and stomach aches!

## fruits

Fresh, seasonal fruits – organically grown – are the best snack and the most delicious dessert! Try buying local fruits more often than exotic kinds that have travelled for weeks and months to get to your supermarket. That said, a banana here-and-there and some exotic fruits in summer can really make a big difference and bring variety and freshness to your diet.

## non-dairy milk

Non-dairy milks are versatile ingredients and can be used in many recipes. Homemade nut milks (page 16) are my favourite, but sometimes unsweetened store-bought soya/soy milk is great for cakes, cookies and other baked goodies.

## tofu & tempeh

Tofu and tempeh are both soy products and if you've been a vegan for a while you should know them quite well. Tofu can be used in some recipes that call for dairy or eggs, like Versatile Vegan Pizza (page 66) or Tofu Scramble (page 35). Tempeh is a high-quality fermented protein made from soya/soy beans, which adds a great aroma and a strong taste to many dishes, especially in winter. It's not necessary to eat tofu and tempeh in large quantities, just an occasional portion here and there.

## condiments

To season my dishes I also often use naturally fermented soy sauce (shoyu or tamari) and unpasteurized miso paste (both lighter and darker varieties): very healthy condiments full of enzymes and rich in nutrients. To make some of the recipes in this book extra tasty, I suggest using organic, additive-free vegetable bouillon powder or cubes, but if you prefer not to, the dish will turn out tasty nevertheless!

Dijon mustard has a space reserved on my fridge shelf. You will find it in many of my marinades and I also use it in sauces for vegetables or in salads. Tomato passata/strained tomatoes and tomato concentrate deepen the taste of some dishes so it's a good idea to have them in stock.

# millet mash

A potato mash counterpart, mashed millet is much richer in nutrients, incredibly tasty and a great side dish to many vegan comforts in this book. It can be made using only millet, but I often add a vegetable, like pumpkin, leek, cauliflower or celeriac/celery root to make the taste even richer and increase vegetable intake.

150–225 g/1–1½ cups pumpkin, leek, cauliflower or celeriac/celery root, if desired
700 ml/3 cups water
200 g/1 cup millet
½ teaspoon sea salt
2 tablespoons olive oil
crushed black pepper

Serves 2-4

If using pumpkin or celeriac/celery root, peel off the skin and cut it into small cubes. If using leeks or cauliflower, wash them well and cut them into small pieces.

Bring the water to the boil in a large saucepan. Wash and drain the millet before adding it to the pan, then wait until the water boils again, before adding the salt and vegetables. Lower the heat, cover, and simmer for about 15 minutes without stirring. Remove the pan from the heat and allow it to sit for 5 minutes. Add the oil and the pepper and mix in.

While the mixture is still hot, use a handheld blender to make a thick mash and serve immediately. In case you have to wait to serve the mash, add a little more hot water or non-dairy milk and blend again before serving.

# homemade seitan

Seitan is a great and inexpensive source of protein. While unseasoned seitan is bland, it has a great ability to soak up marinades, so it's a particularly versatile ingredient.

For the seitan

1 kg/2¼ lbs. unbleached wheat flour
600ml/2½ cups warm water

For the cooking broth

1.2 litres/5 cups water
1 tablespoon bouillon powder
1 teaspoon sweet paprika
1 teaspoon chilli/chile flakes
1 bay leaf
5-cm/2-in. piece of ginger, peeled
½ teaspoon sea salt

Mix the flour and water into a stiff dough and knead for a minute. Place the dough in a large bowl and pour over enough warm water to cover it. Let it soak for 30 minutes and then drain the water. Rinse the dough in running water (alternating hot and cold) in the kitchen sink and knead it until the water coming off the dough is clear rather than milky. The dough will begin to separate during this process, so have a sieve/strainer close by to drain the kneading water, so no gluten tries to run out of the bowl. After 10 minutes, you should be left with a ball of raw gluten weighing about 400–450 g (14–16 oz.).

Add all the broth ingredients to a large pot and bring to a boil. Add the seitan, cover, and simmer for about 40 minutes, then leave it to cool in the cooking liquid. You can use it immediately or refrigerate it (covered with broth) until ready to use (it will keep for 12 days). Pat it dry before slicing and marinating (page 23).

# how to cook brown rice

The rice I use most often is short-grain brown rice, but the cooking method is the same for long-grain brown rice, brown basmati etc. It's best, but not essential, to soak the rice overnight and use the soaking water for cooking.

190 g/1 cup short grain brown rice

480 ml/2 cups water

a few pinches of sea salt

To pressure cook the rice, add the water and rice to the pressure cooker and let it boil; when it begins to boil, add the salt and close with the lid, allowing the pressure to rise. If your pressure cooker isn't heavy-bottomed, use a flame deflector to help distribute the heat more evenly. When the pressure cooker has reached the right pressure, turn down the heat to minimum and cook for 45 minutes. After the pressure goes down, remove the lid, fluff the rice and transfer it into a large bowl.

If you're using a normal saucepan, add the water and rice and let it boil; then add the salt and close with the heaviest lid that you have. There's no need to stir the rice during cooking. However, do be careful not to burn the rice as more moisture evaporates from a normal pot compared to a pressure cooker, so add a few tablespoons of extra water if needed. Cook for 40 minutes, then fluff the rice and transfer into a large bowl.

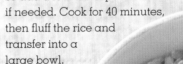

# homemade nut & seed milk

Preparing your own nut or seed milk will save a fortune in the long run, and you'll be consuming a nutritionally superior drink in which all the enzymes remain intact, unlike in store-bought pasteurized milks.

150 g/1 cup nuts or seeds of your choosing
500 ml/2 cups water, for soaking
1 litre/4 cups water, for blending
3 dates or 2 tablespoons rice or agave syrup (optional)
¼ teaspoon bourbon vanilla powder (optional)
*cheese cloth or nut milk bag*

Begin by soaking the nuts or seeds in water overnight. If you're in a hurry you can soak them for an hour or so, but overnight is best. Rinse and drain, discarding the soaking water.

Add the soaked nuts or seeds to your blender (high-speed blenders are most efficient for this), together with the water. Blend for a couple of minutes, until you have a smooth liquid without chunks. Now, use a double-folded cheese cloth or a nut-milk bag and strain the milk over a big bowl or jar. Squeeze really well to extract as much milk as possible. The residue on the cheese cloth or nut-milk bag is nut or seed flour, which you can add to smoothies, raw cakes or cracker dough (but make sure to use it within 2–3 days); alternatively you can dehydrate this flour on a very low temperature in the oven and you'll then be able to use it in bread, cakes and cookie mixes.

Raw nut and seed milk is very mild in flavour so, if you want to enhance the flavour to make it more appealing for children, for example, you can blend in a couple of dates or syrup and some vanilla.

It's best to make the milk fresh and use it immediately, but it will keep in the fridge for up to two days. My favourite milks are: almond milk, hazelnut milk and walnut milk but I also like sunflower and pumpkin seed milk. Hemp seeds make a very popular milk, too!

# nut cheese

Nut and seed cheeses are a great alternative to dairy and if you crave conventional cheese sometimes, this recipe might help you to overcome that! Also, rejuvelac, which you'll be making in the first stage of the recipe, is a great energising drink, so you can make more and enjoy it as an enzyme-rich refreshment when you feel tired.

### For the cheese starter (rejuvelac)

40 g/¼ cup sprouted spelt berries (a tiny white tail is enough)

470 ml/2 cups water

Place the berries and water in a jar, cover with paper towel or a cheese cloth, and store in a warm place for 48 hours, or until the mixture turns fizzy and a little sour. In winter you'll need to either put the mixture close to the radiator, or leave it to ferment for at least a week at room temperature. Drain, keep the liquid and discard the berries. Instead of spelt berries, you can also use rye berries, unhulled millet, buckwheat, and even brown rice.

### For the cheese

270 g/2 cups nuts or seeds, soaked overnight
110 ml/½ cup rejuvelac
¼ teaspoon sea salt
2 garlic cloves, crushed
2 tablespoons olive oil
*cheese cloth*

Drain the nuts and place them in a high-speed blender or food processor. Add the rejuvelac, garlic, salt and oil and blend until completely smooth. Line a sieve/strainer with two layers of cheese cloth, and spoon in the mixture before leaving it to set in a warm place for 24–48 hours. Then, form the mixture into the desired shape (I usually just flip it over from the sieve/strainer onto a plate). Leave it covered with the cheese cloth or peel it off and wrap the plate in clingfilm/plastic wrap. Leave in the refrigerator to finish setting for another day before serving. This is a soft cheese, and will keep in the fridge for about 10 days. Use it with crackers (page 79), bread (page 27), on top of vegetables or use it as a cheese substitute on pizza (page 66), before or after baking – it's up to you! Also, feel free to use herbs and spices in addition to or instead of the garlic; crushed black pepper, oregano, thyme, paprika, etc. all work well.

My favourite combination of nuts is blanched almonds and cashews, but sunflower seeds mixed with cashews work well too, even though the colour isn't completely white. You can also try making this cheese with macadamia nuts.

# soffritto

A very simple way to add flavour to many dishes is by making fragrant soffritto (in Italian 'soffriggere' means 'to fry slowly') by sautéeing aromatic vegetables such as onions, celeriac/celery root, celery and carrots in a heavy-bottomed pan.

5 tablespoons olive oil

90 g/⅔ cup finely diced onion

1 medium carrot, finely diced, or 50 g/½ cup carrot pulp

50 g/½ cup peeled and finely diced celeriac/celery root (or use celery instead)

¼ teaspoon sea salt

3 garlic cloves, crushed

¼ teaspoon dried oregano, thyme or basil

Over a medium heat, in a heavy-bottomed pan, heat the olive oil and add the onion, carrot and celeriac/celery root (or celery). Sprinkle with the salt, stir and cook, covered, for 10–15 minutes or until the vegetables are tender and have released their full aroma. Be careful not to brown them, though. Add the garlic and herbs and sauté for another minute or two. That's it! Try also using (bell) peppers, leeks or fennel to make your soffritto slightly different every time you cook it.

You will notice that I use soffritto in some recipes in this book. Many of my stews, stuffings, ragouts, soups and sauces can thank their full flavour to this simple but essential base of aromatic vegetables, so don't rush the cooking time!

# vegan stuffings

It's fun to fill different types of vegetables, then bake or cook them for a quite impressive and really delicious result! The combination of protein, vegetables and grains makes this type of stuffing a complete meal. I use it to stuff peppers (see page 50), firm tomatoes, courgette/zucchini and aubergine/eggplant, as well as a filling for cabbage rolls, rice-paper rolls or spring rolls.

250 g/9 oz. tofu, seitan or tempeh

50 g/⅓ cup finely diced onion

4 tablespoons sunflower or olive oil

pinch of chilli powder

½ teaspoon ground ginger

¼ teaspoon ground turmeric

1 teaspoon dried herbes de Provence

3 teaspoons soy sauce

300 g/10½ oz.whole grains, cooked (brown rice, millet, quinoa, etc.)

2 tablespoons rolled oats or millet flakes

sea salt and crushed black pepper

Mash the tofu or tempeh with a fork, or, if using seitan, put in a food processor with an S-blade to finely chop it. In a large frying pan/skillet over a low heat, sauté the onion until translucent, then add the dry spices and herbs and cook for a minute more. Add the soy sauce and bring up the heat. After the soy sauce is well incorporated, add the cooked grains and rolled oats or millet flakes and mix everything well before seasoning with salt and pepper to taste. When the stuffing looks like a thick risotto, it's ready for filling. Remember that the mixture will expand a little bit during cooking, so don't overfill the vegetables.

You can always make the stuffing a day or two in advance, as well as freeze it (if using tempeh or seitan, but not tofu) if you have leftovers.

# marinating & frying tofu, seitan & tempeh

To make your stews, ragouts, sauces, curries and other lovely dishes extra yummy, it is very important to marinate and fry tofu, seitan and tempeh properly in advance. This way, each piece soaks up spices and forms a nice crunchy crust. I will be using tofu, seitan and tempeh prepared this way as a base in some other, more complex dishes throughout this cookbook. Adjust spices, herbs and oils to your liking.

290 g/10 oz. tofu, seitan or tempeh, cut in to 2-cm x 2-cm/ ¾-in. x ¾-in. cubes

### For the marinade

4 teaspoons tamari

1 teaspoon oil of your choosing (aromatic oils like olive or dark sesame work best)

2 teaspoons water

2 teaspoons Dijon mustard (optional)

2 teaspoons dried herbs or ground spices of your choosing

2 garlic cloves, crushed

handful of unbleached plain/ all-purpose flour or millet flour, for frying

200 g/1 cup sunflower oil, for deep-frying

Place the tofu, seitan or tempeh cubes in a deep plate. Put all ingredients for the marinade in a small jar, close and shake. Pour this mixture over the cubes and mix well so that all the pieces are covered in the marinade. If the marinade turns out overly thick, add 1–2 teaspoons of extra water, just to make it runny enough to cover all the cubes. Cover with clingfilm/ plastic wrap and let it sit at room temperature for at least 30 minutes. You can also do this a day in advance and let it sit in the fridge.

Put a little flour in a bowl and roll each cube separately in it. Be sure to coat the sides of each the cube with flour, but be careful not to wipe the marinade off. It's also important that the layer of flour is thin, so remove any excess by shaking each cube between the palms of your hands.

Layer a tray or a big plate with paper towels, which you'll use to drain the tofu, seitan or tempeh after frying it. I use a small pot and deep-fry the prepared cubes in a few batches, but if you want you can fry them all at once in a big pan – just make sure you don't overcrowd it! The oil is ready for frying when it starts bubbling once you drop a piece of tofu, seitan or tempeh in it. Fry the cubes for 1–2 minutes, until golden brown, then drain on the paper towels before using in other recipes. However, you could snack on these cubes as they are, or add them to a salad instead of croutons or make quick skewers, adding pieces of raw or baked vegetables.

# two types of pizza dough

Depending on your preferences of flour and leavening agents and the time you have at your disposal, I'm offering you two types of pizza dough to choose from. Both are tasty and develop a thin crust on the edges during baking.

## Basic yeast dough

*For the starter*

40 g/¼ cup rye flour

55 ml/¼ cup lukewarm water

2 teaspoons active dry yeast (additive-free)

*For the dough*

200 g/1½ cups unbleached spelt flour, plus extra for kneading

30 g/¼ cup wholemeal/ whole wheat flour

½ teaspoon sea salt

110 ml /½ cup lukewarm water

1 tablespoon olive oil

1 tablespoon soy milk

40-cm x 32-cm/16-in. x 12½-in. baking pan, well oiled

### Makes one 29-cm/11½-in. diameter pizza

## Basic yeast-free dough

240 g/1¾ cups unbleached plain/all-purpose flour or millet flour (for gluten-free pizza)

1½ teaspoons aluminium-free baking powder

½ teaspoon sea salt

2 tablespoons olive oil

110 ml/½ cup lukewarm water

40-cm x 32-cm/16-in. x 12½-in. baking pan, well oiled

### Makes one 27-cm/10½-in. diameter pizza

## Basic yeast dough

Mix together all the starter ingredients in a bowl, cover and allow it to rest for 30 minutes. For the dough, mix together the flours and salt in another bowl. In a jug/pitcher, mix together the water, oil and milk, then add the starter ingredients and mix well. Finally, add the contents of the jug/pitcher to your dry ingredients in the bowl and mix with a wooden spoon.

Place the dough on a lightly floured work surface and knead for a couple of minutes (adding flour as you do so) until it is soft and slightly sticky. Put the dough into a large oiled bowl and rub a little oil on the surface of the dough, too. Cover the bowl with a damp tea/dish towel and allow to rise for 2½ hours in a warm place. Punch the dough down and allow it to rise for another 45 minutes. Preheat the oven to 240°C (475°F) Gas 9. Place a piece of parchment paper on your work surface and use a rolling pin to gently flatten the dough into a 29-cm/11½-in. circle. Transfer onto the baking pan and sprinkle on your chosen toppings. Lower the oven temperature to 220°C (425°F) Gas 7 and bake on the bottom surface of the oven for 12–15 minutes.

## Basic yeast-free dough

In a bowl, mix together the flour, baking powder and salt. Add the oil and use a whisk to incorporate it into the flour. Slowly add the water and knead the mixture with your hand until you get a soft but firm dough. Place on a work surface (adding flour only if the dough is sticky, which will depend on the type of flour you're using) and knead for a couple of minutes. Wrap the dough in clingfilm/plastic wrap and let it rest for 30 minutes at room temperature. Preheat the oven to 240°C (475°F) Gas 9. Unwrap the dough, place in the middle of a sheet of parchment paper and use a rolling pin to gently flatten the dough into a 27-cm/ 10½-in. circle. Transfer onto the baking pan and sprinkle on your chosen toppings. Lower the oven temperature to 220°C (425°F) Gas 7 and bake on the bottom surface of the oven for 12–15 minutes.

# gluten-free bread

One of many variations of my favourite bread, this lovely loaf is both gluten-free and yeast-free, so you don't need to knead it or wait for it to rise and it stays fresh for a couple of days! If you make nut milk (page 16) and have leftover flours (see nut milk recipe on page 16) you can use it here, too, as it will give this bread a nice texture and a nutty flavour. Also, try using beer instead of sparkling water for a 'yeasty' smell and taste.

110 g/1 cup millet flakes

350 g/2½ cups millet flour

3 teaspoons aluminium-free baking powder

1½ teaspoons sea salt

450 ml/1¾ cups sparkling mineral water (or use beer instead)

1 tablespoon olive oil

1 teaspoon apple cider vinegar

2 tablespoons seeds of your choosing (pumpkin, sesame, sunflower, etc.)

500-g/1-lb. loaf pan (23 cm x 12 cm/9 in. x 4¾ in.)

oven thermometer (optional)

### Makes about 14 slices

### For the croutons

3 slices Gluten-free Bread (see recipe above)

3 tablespoons olive oil

2 tablespoons water

¼ teaspoon sea salt or tamari

1 teaspoon dried herbs of your choosing

23-cm x 30-cm/ 9-in. x 12-in. baking pan, well-oiled

### Serves 3

Preheat the oven to 220°C (425°F) Gas 7.

Stir together the millet flakes, flour, baking powder and salt in a bowl until well mixed. In a separate bowl, whisk together the sparkling water (or beer) with the olive oil. Pour this into the dry ingredients, mixing vigorously with a spatula until you get a medium-thick batter.

In order to get a nicely shaped loaf, cut a sheet of parchment paper to fit inside the loaf pan without any creases. Sprinkle with 1 tablespoon of the seeds. Pour the dough into the pan and top with the remaining seeds.

Put the pan into the preheated oven, lower the temperature to 200°C (400°F) Gas 6 and bake for 1 hour. Use an oven thermometer if you're not sure about the exact temperature in the oven.

Remove from the oven and tip the bread out of the pan, peel off the paper and allow it to cool completely on a wire rack. This will prevent the bread from absorbing moisture and will keep the crust crisp. Wrap the bread in tea/dish towels and store in a cool, dry place for up to 5 days.

To make croutons, preheat the oven to 180°C (350°F) Gas 4. Cut the bread into small cubes. Mix the other ingredients in a large bowl and pour them over the bread cubes, making sure that each one is coated. Spread the cubes onto a baking pan and put it in the oven until the croutons turn golden brown and crispy, around 30 minutes. Check them every 5 minutes and stir them around to ensure that they bake evenly. Don't worry if they are a little soft when removing them from the oven – the croutons will dry as they cool down.

Note: adding more oil to the crouton mixture makes for a richer taste and more crunchiness.

# breakfast & brunch

# alkalizing green juice

Make a commitment to your health goals and get a cold-press juicer. It will change your life! Starting the day with a glass of freshly squeezed veggie and fruit elixir will make you feel energized, nourished and light.

5–6 medium Granny Smith or other apples

380 g/13 oz. or 1 small head organic cabbage

2 medium pomegranates

4 handfuls of green leafy vegetables (kale, chard, spinach, carrot greens, parsley, nettles, etc.)

½ organic lemon

15 g/½ oz. fresh ginger

about 360 ml/1½ cups water

1 teaspoon flaxseed, hemp or other oil

Makes 1.4 litres/1¼ quarts

Wash all the fruit and vegetables. Slice the apples (leave the skin and pips) and cabbage. Cut and break the pomegranates into segments. Next, divide the seeds from their membranes. Peel the lemon and ginger and begin juicing all the ingredients (except the water). Add a little of the water from time to time (it's always a good idea to dilute pure juice with ¼ to ⅓ part water to get an isotonic, rehydrating drink). Add the oil to the juice (this will allow all the oil-soluble vitamins to be absorbed), stir and serve immediately. If you have leftover juice, keep it refrigerated and drink it within 12 hours.

# raw cocoa milkshake

A combination of cocoa and greens, this milkshake will not only give you energy but also a considerable amount of chlorophyll, which displays antioxidant and anti-inflammatory properties, in addition to being a good source of magnesium.

500 ml/2 cups Nut Milk (page 16)

1 tablespoon raw cocoa powder

6 soft dates or 1 very ripe banana, peeled

¼ teaspoon bourbon vanilla powder

2 large handfuls of green leafy vegetables (dark kale, spinach, chard, etc.)

Serves 1–2

Add all the ingredients to the blender jug and blend until completely smooth and foamy (a high-speed blender is the best option to achieve a velvety consistency). Taste the mixture and adjust according to your liking: to make it sweeter, add a couple more dates; add more cocoa powder for an extra kick of flavour and energy. Depending on the season, adding fresh strawberries, blueberries, apples or other sweet fruits will make the shake taste slightly different (but still great) every day!

# carrot juice with beets & pomegranate

I'm always trying to introduce more iron-rich foods into my diet. Beet(root) is full of iron but it is strong-tasting, so I like to combine it with other fruits and veggies to camouflage its earthy aroma. Carrots are a good juice base, and pomegranates serve here as a great C vitamin source, enabling the iron to be absorbed in the body more easily.

6 medium carrots

2 medium beet(root)

2 medium pomegranates

230 ml/1 cup water

1 teaspoon flaxseed oil

Serves 1-2

Wash and slice the carrots and beet(root), without peeling. Cut and segment the pomegranates, dividing the seeds from the membranes. Start juicing, adding a little of the water from time to time. Add the oil to the juice, stir and serve immediately.

If you have leftover juice, keep it refrigerated and drink within 12 hours. If pomegranates are out of season, use oranges or lemons instead. Red cabbage works well instead of beet(root), and will give this juice a fluorescent purple glow.

# coconut & strawberry frappé

Coconut water is a great source of electrolytes necessary for proper hydration. I sometimes treat myself with a carton of raw organic coconut water and use it in frappés, smoothies and milkshakes. Combined with freshly made nut milk, ripe strawberries and a couple of dates, this frappé will make you feel happy and hydrated!

250 ml/1 cup raw organic coconut water

460 ml/2 cups Nut Milk (page 16)

400 g/3 cups fresh strawberries

1 tablespoon nut butter

8 soft dates

few drops of lemon juice

Serves 2

Place all ingredients into the blender jar, and mix until completely smooth and foamy. Drink immediately!

You can use any other fresh fruits you want, and add cocoa powder, spices and other dried fruits to make it sweeter. Raspberries, blackberries, apples or ripe apricots also make a great combination with the nut milk and coconut water.

# tofu scramble

I've never heard of anybody disliking this yummy way of using tofu, and former egg-lovers are especially keen on it since it looks and tastes very similar to scrambled eggs. Actually, way better than scrambled eggs! As you can use many different types of vegetables, herbs and spices, this is just one suggestion for springtime, when asparagus (wild and cultivated) is abundant at farmers' markets. I use a big cast-iron wok to make this dish, but you can also use a heavy-bottomed frying pan/skillet.

150 g/2 cups fresh shiitake mushrooms

4 tablespoons olive oil

120 g/1 cup onions sliced into thin half-moons

½ teaspoon sea salt

80 g/1 cup trimmed asparagus, sliced diagonally at the bottom (if using wild asparagus, then only use the soft tops)

2 tablespoons tamari

½ teaspoon ground turmeric

300 g/10 oz. fresh tofu, mashed with a fork

4 tablespoons water, if necessary

1 teaspoon dark sesame oil

½ teaspoon dried basil or 2 tablespoons chopped fresh basil

crushed black pepper

*Serves 2–3*

Cut the mushrooms in half lengthways, then cut into thinner wedges. Add the olive oil, onions and salt to the wok or frying pan/skillet and sauté over a medium heat briefly, stirring energetically to prevent sticking.

Add the mushrooms, asparagus, tamari and turmeric and continue stirring with two wooden spoons. When the mushrooms have soaked up a bit of tamari, turn up the heat, add the tofu and stir for another 1–2 minutes. The scramble should be uniformly yellow in colour. At this point you can add the water to make the scramble juicy, and continue cooking for a couple more minutes. However, whether you need water or not depends on how soft your tofu was to begin with – softer types are moist and don't need any water at the end of cooking.

Mix in the dark sesame oil and basil, season with pepper and serve warm, with a nice salad and a few slices of toasted homemade bread.

# simple & filling chia seed porridge

The shiny chia seeds have recently been rediscovered and are referred to as 'an ancient American superfood'. Rich in calcium and omega-3 and -6 fatty acids, they are nutritionally very similar to flax and sesame seeds, and should therefore become part of everybody's diet. This quick porridge will fill your tummy for many hours!

40 g/¼ cup chia seeds

2 tablespoons raisins or other dried fruits

230 ml/1 scant cup Nut Milk (page 16)

pinch of sea salt

⅛ teaspoon bourbon vanilla powder or ground cinnamon

2 tablespoons raw or dry-roasted mixed nuts

fresh fruit, chopped (optional)

*Serves 1*

In a bowl, mix the chia seeds and dried fruits. Lightly warm the nut milk in a small saucepan, add the salt and vanilla or cinnamon, and pour it over the seeds and leave it to soak for 10 minutes.

If you only have raw nuts, preheat the oven to 180°C (350° F) Gas 4, spread the nuts on a tray and roast for 10–14 minutes, stirring occasionally. When the nuts start cracking and releasing their oils, that's when they're done. Be careful not to burn them, as this can happen easily, so it's best to check how they're doing after 8–10 minutes and continue roasting for a couple more minutes if they're not done. Transfer them onto a plate and wait for them to cool slightly. Chop them coarsely and sprinkle over the porridge, along with a little chopped fresh fruit, if desired.

Dry-roasted nuts are great as a healthy snack and as an addition to cakes, cookies, salads – to anything really!

# pure energy bars

There is always a stash of these bars in my fridge, each neatly wrapped up and ready to go! They are amazing for breakfast, as a pick-me-up snack or a guilt-free dessert. You can use millet flakes to make these bars gluten-free and any other dried fruits instead of apricots. Also, try adding orange juice and zest instead of lemon for the popular cocoa-orange combo.

2 very ripe bananas

3 tablespoons extra virgin coconut oil

zest of 1 organic lemon plus 1 tablespoon lemon juice

15 unsulphured dried apricots, diced

1 teaspoon rum (optional)

200 g/2¼ cups fine rolled oats

¼ teaspoon ground cinnamon

⅛ teaspoon bourbon vanilla powder

3 tablespoons raw cocoa powder

pinch of sea salt

18-cm x 18-cm/ 7-in. x 7-in. shallow dish or baking pan

Makes 8 bars

Peel the bananas and put them in a deep plate before mashing them thoroughly with a fork. If the coconut oil has solidified, set the jar in a bowl of boiling water until the oil begins to liquify. Add the oil, lemon zest and juice apricots and rum, if using, to the mashed bananas and stir well. In a large bowl, combine the rolled oats, cinnamon, vanilla, cocoa and salt. Mix and add the banana mash to the dry ingredients. Use a spatula to combine the ingredients really well – there should be no dry patches of oats and the dough should be thick and sticky.

Now take the dish or small baking pan and cover its bottom and sides with clingfilm/plastic wrap. Place the dough in it and use a spatula or your hands to press down the mixture until you get an even layer about 1.5 cm/½ in. thick. Wrap well with more clingfilm/plastic wrap and refrigerate for at least 2 hours (but best if left overnight). Unwrap the clingfilm/plastic wrap and cut into 8 even bars; wrap each one separately and use up during the week!

# fried tofu sandwiches

A good-quality vegan sandwich can be eaten for breakfast, lunch or dinner, and if the ingredients are well chosen, you'll be getting all the necessary nutrients. The three main components of a satisfying sandwich are: tasty bread, seasoned protein and freshly pickled vegetables – the combinations are endless!

### For the filling

240 g/8¼ oz. tofu, seitan or tempeh, marinated and fried (see page 23)

4 tablespoons spread of your choosing (Sunflower Seed & Cashew Mayonnaise, page 103, Aubergine/Eggplant & Date Chutney, page 108, Roasted Red Pepper Dip, page 108)

sliced pickles or kimchi, to taste

2 handfuls of lettuce or other salad greens

4 tablespoons seed sprouts

### Serves 2

Follow the instructions on how to make Gluten-free Bread on page 27, but halve all the ingredients. Use the same-sized loaf pan as indicated in the recipe, as this way you will get a shallower loaf that you can cut crossways and make 2 big sandwiches from. Let the loaf cool completely before cutting.

To prepare the tofu, seitan or tempeh, cut four 10-cm x 6-cm/ 4-in x 2½-in. slices, 6-mm/¼-in. thick. Marinate and fry these slices following the instructions in the recipe on page 21. You don't have to deep-fry the slices; just cover the bottom of the pan with oil and fry them on both sides until browned.

When the loaf has cooled, cut it crossways in the middle, then lengthways to get 2 sandwiches. First add the spread on the bottom slices, then add 2 slices of fried tofu, seitan or tempeh, sprinkle with pickles, salad and seed sprouts and top with the remaining slices of bread.

Eat immediately or wrap in clingfilm/plastic wrap and eat when you're hungry!

# spicy potato strudel

*Everybody loves potatoes and everybody loves crunchy filo/phyllo pastry, so this is a safe recipe for picky eaters and vegan-sceptical guests as it's a real crowd pleaser!*

6 filo/phyllo dough sheets
(35 cm x 30 cm/13¾ in. x 12 in.)

150 ml/⅔ cup water

90 g/scant ½ cup sunflower oil

4 large potatoes, peeled

180 g/1½ cups onions, diced

¼ teaspoon sea salt

¼–½ teaspoon crushed black pepper

1½ teaspoons vegetable bouillon powder

23-cm x 30-cm/9-in. x 12-in. baking pan, well oiled

**Makes 12 pieces**

Take the filo/phyllo sheets out of the fridge 30 minutes before making the strudel. This will prevent the leaves from cracking during baking. Place one sheet of filo/phyllo on a dry work surface, with the longer side facing you (keep the remaining filo/phyllo sheets covered with clingfilm/plastic wrap to prevent them from drying out). In a small bowl, mix 3 tablespoons of the water and 4 tablespoons of the oil (taken from the amounts listed). With a silicone spatula, brush the sheet lightly with the oil and water mixture. Top it with another sheet of filo/phyllo dough (the second one doesn't need oiling).

Dice 2 potatoes, and grate the other two. In a large bowl, mix the potatoes with the onions, salt and pepper. Divide the mixture into 3 equal portions (each should weigh about 220 g/7¾ oz.).

Preheat the oven to 180°C (350°F) Gas 4. Boil the remaining water and add the bouillon powder.

Spread 1 portion of the potato filling on the bottom edge of the 2 filo/phyllo sheets in a 6-cm/2½-in. wide strip, leaving a 2-cm/¾-in. edge on the sides to prevent the filling from falling out. Roll carefully into a nice strudel and place it in the pre-oiled baking pan. Repeat with the remaining sheets and filling to make 3 strudels. Brush them with oil and use a sharp knife to cut partially through the dough, marking 4 slices per strudel. Splash 2 spoons of hot bouillon over each strudel. Put the pan in the oven and bake for 10 minutes. Pour over some bouillon again and repeat until you have no liquid left. This strudel will need another 25–30 minutes to turn brown and crispy on the top and edges, but soft and juicy in the middle. Serve warm or cold, with a salad or a glass of non-dairy yogurt.

# salty onion pancakes

When I'm out of home-baked bread and need something to go with a soup or stew, these are great! Full of onion flavour, slightly crispy on the outside and a little chewy when you bite into them, onion pancakes can also be served with dips, sauces and salads.

200 g/1½ cups unbleached plain/all-purpose flour or millet or wholemeal/whole wheat flour

110 ml/½ cup boiling water

3 teaspoons cold water

2 tablespoons olive oil plus extra for brushing and frying

70 g/¾ cup onions, thinly sliced

¼ teaspoon dried oregano

3 spring onions/scallions, washed and chopped

1 tablespoon dark sesame oil

1 teaspoon sea salt

Serves 2

Add the flour to a bowl and pour in the boiling water. Mix well, add the cold water and stir until the dough is evenly moistened. Place the dough onto a lightly floured work surface and knead until smooth, which will take about 4 minutes. Dust the surface and your hands with more flour if necessary, to prevent sticking. Wrap the dough in clingfilm/plasic wrap and let it rest at room temperature for 30 minutes.

In a frying pan/skillet, heat the olive oil and sauté the sliced onions with a pinch of salt and the dried oregano until they're soft and fragrant. Remove the onions from heat and mix in the spring onions/scallions, dark sesame oil and salt.

Divide the dough into 4 equal pieces. Roll each into a 15-cm/6-in. circular pancake and brush each one with a little oil.

Divide the onion mixture between the 4 pieces and spread it into the dough. Next, coil each piece of dough into a snail shape and tuck the end underneath. Now, with the help of a rolling pin, press on top of the 'snail', rolling it into a circular pancake shape again, about 5 mm/⅕ in. thick. Repeat with the other 3 pieces of dough. Heat a pancake pan (cast-iron is best) over a medium heat. Sprinkle with 1 teaspoon olive oil for each pancake, and fry on both sides until slightly golden. Slice each pancake into 4 triangles before serving. Serve with stews, soups, spreads and salads.

# mains & comfort food

# delicious tofu curry & chapatis

*This is my favourite curry recipe and I almost always overeat when I make it! Make sure you marinate and fry the tofu first as I suggest - it makes a big difference to the taste and texture. I often serve this to guests and everybody falls in love with it.*

290 g/10 oz. fresh tofu, cut into 2-cm x 2-cm/¾-in. x ¾-in. cubes

5 tablespoons sunflower, coconut or olive oil

180 g/1½ cups diced onions

2 tablespoons finely grated fresh ginger

4 garlic cloves, crushed

2 teaspoons curry powder (or curry paste or your own spice blend)

¼–½ teaspoon chilli powder

1 teaspoon ground turmeric

1 tablespoon tomato purée/paste

½ teaspoon sea salt

300 ml/1¼ cups water

1 teaspoon kuzu, ground arrowroot or cornflour/cornstarch

2 tablespoons freshly chopped coriander/cilantro, chives or parsley, to garnish

### For the chapatis

150 g/1 cup wholemeal/whole wheat flour

150 g/1 cup unbleached plain/all-purpose flour

½ teaspoon sea salt

2 tablespoons sunflower oil

140 ml/½ cup plus 1 tablespoon lukewarm water

*Serves 2–3*

To prepare the tofu, refer to the instructions on page 23, and for the 2 teaspoons of dry herbs or powdered spices of your choosing, add 1 teaspoon curry powder, ½ teaspoon powdered coriander seeds and ½ teaspoon ground cumin. Marinate and fry the tofu as instructed.

Heat the oil in a large (lidded) frying pan/skillet and fry the onions, ginger and garlic over a medium heat until fragrant. Add all the spices, the tomato purée/paste and salt and stir until slightly brown. Stir in the marinated fried tofu, then add the water and cover with the lid. Bring to the boil, stir again, lower the heat and cook for 5–10 minutes. You can add more water if you like your curry more stew-like. At the end, dilute the kuzu, arrowroot or cornflour/cornstarch in a little cold water and add it to the curry, stirring until it boils again. Your delicious curry is now done! Garnish with your choice of herbs and serve with freshly cooked basmati rice and/or chapatis (see below).

In a bowl, mix together the flours, salt and oil with a balloon whisk. Start adding the water and kneading the mixture until it forms a smooth, medium-soft dough. Kneading is crucial, so do not skip this, and continue kneading until you get a smooth, pliable dough (add a bit more flour or water if necessary). Wrap in clingfilm/plastic wrap and set aside for 15 minutes to rest.

Divide the dough into 10 equal portions and, on a work surface, roll the dough into smooth balls. Dust each ball of dough with flour, then using a rolling pin, roll them out into discs about 13 cm/5 in. in diameter. Dust with more flour if needed to prevent the dough from sticking to your work surface.

Heat a cast-iron or stainless-steel frying pan/skillet over a medium heat until hot. Add one of the dough discs and flip it over when bumps appear on the surface; keep an eye on it, as it shouldn't actually brown. Leave it until bumps appear again, then flip it over one last time and leave it in the pan for a moment. Gently press the chapati around its edges with an oven glove/mitt and it should puff up in the middle! Cook the remaining chapatis in the same way. Serve them immediately.

# stuffed Babura peppers in sauce

This dish is the ultimate comfort food of my childhood. In some families stuffed peppers are baked, but women in my family have always boiled them in sauce, making them especially juicy and full of flavour. Vegan stuffed peppers taste equally good and are much healthier than their non-vegan counterparts!

1 portion Vegan Stuffing (page 20)

7 Babura peppers (see Note)

230 ml/1 cup tomato passata/strained tomatoes

1 litre/4 cups water

2 bay leaves

1 teaspoon sea salt

1–2 tablespoons kuzu, arrowroot powder or cornflour/cornstarch (optional)

2 tablespoons chopped fresh parsley, to garnish

20-cm/8-in. diameter saucepan

Serves 3–4

Gently cut off the caps of the peppers and seed them. Fill each with about 100 g/⅔ cup of the stuffing. Arrange the cut side of the peppers so that they face upwards in saucepan (if the pan is narrower, the peppers will not fit; if it's wider, the peppers will flip to the side and the stuffing will fall out during cooking). Add the passata/strained tomatoes and just enough of the water to cover the peppers, followed by the bay leaves and salt. Cover with a lid and bring the pan to a slow boil; then turn the heat down to a simmer until the peppers are soft, which should be about 25 minutes. With the help of a serving spoon, gently take out each pepper and serve them on plates, leaving the sauce in the pan over a medium heat, and slowly add the kuzu, arrowroot powder or cornflour/cornstarch if required (diluted in cold water), whisking vigorously until the desired thickness is reached. I sometimes leave the sauce runny, without thickening it, but it's up to you. Serve a ladleful of the sauce over each portion of peppers, and garnish with the chopped parsley. My favourite side dishes with stuffed peppers are Potato Mash (page 75) or Millet Mash (page 14).

Note: in case you cannot find Babura peppers – the best kind for stuffing because their skin is thinner and they are smaller than regular (bell) peppers – you can use (bell) peppers of any colour. Just bear in mind that (bell) peppers are bigger, will take in more filling and need to cook for a bit longer. You'll also have to determine the size of pan to use to fit them tightly and prevent them from falling over.

# seitan & mushroom goulash

Nothing can beat a plate of hot goulash and creamy gnocchi on a chilly day to comfort and nourish my body and soul. Occasionally I make this dish with just mushrooms, if I don't have seitan, and sometimes I use tempeh or tofu instead. You can serve it over Vegan Gnocchi (page 75), Brown Rice (page 15), Millet Mash (page 14), Potato Mash (page 75) or just plain polenta.

## For the seitan

290 g/2 cups seitan, cut into
2-cm x 2-cm/¾-in. x ¾-in. cubes

## For the goulash

10 g/½ cup dried porcini mushrooms or other dried mushrooms

375 ml/1½ cups water

5 tablespoons sunflower or sesame oil

160 g/1¼ cups onions, diced

½ teaspoon sea salt

½ teaspoon ground dried rosemary

2 bay leaves

1 teaspoon sweet paprika

⅛–¼ teaspoon crushed black pepper or chilli powder

tamari, to taste

80 ml/⅓ cup cooking wine

1½ teaspoons kuzu, arrowroot powder or cornflour/cornstarch

2 tablespoons chopped fresh parsley or spring onion/scallion, to garnish

cooked brown rice (page 15), to serve

**Serves 2–3**

To prepare the seitan, follow the instructions in the recipe on page 23, and for the 2 teaspoons of dry herbs or powdered spices of your choosing, add 1 teaspoon rosemary, ½ teaspoon sweet paprika and ½ teaspoon black pepper. Marinate and fry the seitan as instructed.

Soak the mushrooms in the water for 30 minutes. Drain them, but save the soaking water for later. Next, chop the mushrooms.

Heat the oil in a large frying pan/skillet and sauté the onions with the salt over a medium heat until soft. Add all the herbs and spices and the tamari and stir until everything is slightly browned. Add the mushrooms and stir for another 1–2 minutes. Pour in the wine and let it simmer for another minute. Now stir in the fried seitan cubes, and then add the soaking water and cover. Let the mixture boil, and then stir again, before lowering to a medium heat for 5–10 minutes. At the end, dilute the kuzu, arrowroot powder or cornflour/cornstarch in a little cold water and add it to the goulash, stirring until it boils again. Serve over your choice of side, sprinkled with the chopped parsley or spring onion/scallion.

# spicy burgers & wedges

Whenever I make vegan burgers, people bombard me with questions: how come they don't fall apart or soak up oil; how do I achieve the fine crust and the juicy inside; what's the secret ingredient that makes them so tasty? Making a good vegan burger is a tricky business, but this recipe is the answer! As an ideal accompaniment, these baked sweet potato wedges are a much healthier alternative to fries.

80 g/¾ cup vegetable pulp or grated vegetables (page 10)

50 g/⅓ cup finely diced onion

3 garlic cloves, crushed

1 teaspoon barbecue spice mix

¼ teaspoon sweet paprika

¼ teaspoon ground turmeric

⅛ teaspoon chilli powder

4 tablespoons finely chopped herbs (parsley, chives, etc.)

575 g/3⅓ cups cooked brown rice (page 15), room temperature

¾ teaspoon sea salt

plain/all-purpose flour, for coating

sunflower oil, for frying

pickles, red onion slices and Tofu Mayonnaise (page 103), to serve

### For the sweet potato wedges

2 large sweet potatoes, peeled and cut into wedges

4 tablespoons sunflower oil

¼ teaspoon sweet paprika

½ teaspoon dried oregano

sea salt and crushed black pepper

Serves 4–5

For the burgers, put all the ingredients (except the flour and the oil) in a big bowl. Using your hands, knead the rice into the mixture until everything is well combined and the rice starts becoming sticky. This will prevent the burgers from falling apart or absorbing too much oil. Taste and add more salt and spice if needed – the burgers are usually the spicier part of a meal, so you don't want them to be bland. Allow the mixture to rest for 30 minutes.

With moist hands start shaping the mixture into small, neat burgers – you should be able to make about 14. Roll each burger in a little flour and set aside.

Meanwhile, fill a deep, heavy-bottomed frying pan/skillet with 3 cm/1¼ in. vegetable oil and heat it until the oil starts moving. To tell if it's the right temperature, throw a small piece of the mixture into the pan: if it immediately starts boiling, it's ready to go. Deep-fry a couple of burgers at a time, depending on the size of your pan – it should not be overcrowded. When they turn golden brown, remove them from the oil with a slotted spoon and place them on paper towels. They should be golden with a thin crust and a juicy inside, and should only grease your fingers lightly.

Preheat the oven to 200°C (400°F) Gas 6. Cook the potatoes in a pan of boiling water for 5 minutes. Drain and dry them well. In a small jar, place the remaining ingredients, close and shake, then pour over the wedges until they're well coated. Line a baking sheet with foil, place a roasting rack on top and arrange the wedges on the rack. Bake in the oven for about 20–25 minutes until browned and crispy.

Serve the burgers hot with the wedges, pickles, onion slices and mayonnaise. Enjoy!

# Macedonia-style baked beans

*Creamy, satisfying, comforting, warming – these are just a few adjectives that I associate with this dish. Wait, there's one more – perfect! Typically eaten in colder months, I also prepare it in summer, since I love eating beans made this way!*

340 g/2 cups dried haricot/navy beans

130 g/3 small carrots, cut into bite-sized pieces

4 dried tomato halves

2 small chilli/chile peppers

small piece of kombu seaweed

2 bay leaves

3 small onions

3 garlic cloves

4 tablespoons olive oil

¼ teaspoon sea salt

1 tablespoon sweet paprika powder

1 teaspoon vegetable bouillon powder

½ teaspoon dried oregano

2 tablespoons soy sauce

1 tablespoon apple cider vinegar

2 tablespoons plain/all-purpose flour

sea salt

pressure cooker (optional)

casserole dish, about 35 cm x 25 cm/14 in. x 10 in.

Serves 3-4

Soak the beans in plenty of cold water overnight. Discard the soaking water, place the beans in a pot and add enough water to cover them by 4 cm/1½ in. Add the carrots, tomatoes, chilli peppers, kombu seaweed and bay leaves and, if you're using a pressure cooker, follow the manufacturer's instructions to bring to high pressure, then lower the heat to a minimum for 50–60 minutes. If you are using a normal pot, bring to a boil and skim off any foam, then reduce the heat to medium, half-cover and simmer for 60–90 minutes or until tender, adding cold water occasionally to keep the beans from drying out.

While the beans are cooking, finely chop 2 of the onions and chop the third onion into rings, which you'll need to put aside. Heat the olive oil in heavy-bottomed pan, add the 2 finely chopped onions and a pinch of salt and sauté until the onions are translucent. Add the garlic, paprika, bouillon powder and oregano and fry for 1–2 minutes. Then add the soy sauce, vinegar and flour and whisk vigorously to combine the ingredients and lightly fry the flour, which gives a nice taste as well as texture to this bean dish.

Preheat the oven to 200°C (400°F) Gas 6. When the beans are tender and creamy, remove the bay leaves and chillies/chiles (or leave the chillies/chiles in, if you prefer really spicy baked beans). Add the sautéed onion mixture to the beans and stir well over a high heat until well incorporated. Add salt to taste. The stew should be a little thicker than ordinary stew, and creamy. Pour it into the casserole dish and decorate with the onion rings all over the surface. Bake, uncovered, for 30–40 minutes until a thin crust forms and the onions turn golden brown. Serve warm with bread, chapatis (page 49) or tortillas (page 62) and a nice salad.

# Mediterranean green lentil loaf

*Rich in texture and flavour, this is an ideal choice when your vegan-sceptic friends are visiting for dinner! The lentil and vegetable mixture can be eaten just like that, but it's richer, crispier and more satisfying when baked.*

450 ml/1⅓ cups cold water

200 g/1 cup dried green lentils, washed and drained

2 bay leaves

4-cm/1½-in. strip of kombu seaweed

½ teaspoon sea salt

3 handfuls of chard, spinach or young kale

5 tablespoons olive oil

90 g/¾ cup chopped onion

6 garlic cloves, crushed

½ teaspoon ground dried rosemary or dried herbes de Provence

2 teaspoons Dijon mustard

2 teaspoons lemon juice

30 g/½ cup almond flour (dried leftovers from making almond milk on pages 16–17) or 30 g/⅓ cup fine breadcrumbs, plus extra for sprinkling

crushed black pepper

12-cm x 15-cm/4¾ in. x 6 in. loaf pan, well oiled

Serves 4

In a large saucepan, pour the water over the lentils, add the bay leaves and kombu and put on a high heat to boil, uncovered. When the water boils, add 110 ml/½ cup cold water, then reduce the heat to medium, half-cover and continue cooking for about 10 minutes. Add another 110 ml/½ cup cold water, cover the pan fully and simmer for 10 more minutes. Add a final 110 ml/½ cup cold water, cover and simmer for another 10 minutes. The lentils should by now be soft and a little sticky, with no uncooked parts. Add the salt, then take out the bay leaves and kombu, chop up the kombu into small pieces and stir it into the lentils. Blanch the greens in boiling water for a couple of minutes and then drain and chop them.

Heat the olive oil in a frying pan/skillet over a medium heat and then add garlic, onion, the dried herbs and pepper, to taste. Sauté for a few minutes, then add the blanched greens, cooked lentils, mustard and lemon juice. Mix everything together and then add the flour or breadcrumbs.

Preheat the oven to 200°C (400°F) Gas 6. Add the lentil mix to the oiled loaf pan, making the loaf as high and long as you want. It doesn't have to fill the entire pan. Oil the top with the help of a silicone brush, sprinkle with a little almond flour or a few breadcrumbs and bake for about 30 minutes or until a nice crispy crust forms and the top surface turns golden brown. Let it cool for 20 minutes, then take a big plate and cover the pan with it. With a quick movement, flip the loaf onto the plate. It should retain the shape of the pan. Carefully slice the loaf into thick slices and serve. You can also spoon the mixture out of the pan and serve it like that, if you prefer.

Serve slices of this loaf with Onion Gravy (page 104), Millet Mash (page 14) and a big bowl of garden salad.

# lentil moussaka

For a little while during my late teens I lived in Greece, and their culinary specialities knocked me off my feet! However, as you might know, moussaka is not a vegetable dish, but I watched how the original is made and created my own, vegan version of it.

### For the lentil layer

300 g/1½ cups dried brown lentils, washed and drained

750 ml/3 cups cold water

6-cm/2½-in. strip of kombu seaweed

1 bay leaf

### For the potato & aubergine/eggplant layer

2 large aubergines/eggplants

1 teaspoon sea salt

650 g/1 lb. 7 oz. medium potatoes

100 g/½ cup sunflower oil, for frying

350 ml/1½ cups Strong-flavoured Tomato Sauce (page 99) or Mock Tomato Sauce (page 100)

### For the béchamel topping

50 g/¼ cup olive oil

4 tablespoons millet flour or unbleached plain/all-purpose flour

580 ml/2½ cups soya/soy milk

1 tablespoon white miso (optional)

1 teaspoon sea salt

pinch of ground nutmeg

crushed black pepper, to taste

23-cm x 30-cm/ 9-in. x 12-in. baking pan, well-oiled

Serves 4–6

Cover the lentils with the water, add the kombu and bay leaf and bring to a boil, uncovered. Half-cover and simmer over a medium heat for about 15 minutes. Add another 110 ml/½ cup cold water and simmer for 20 minutes. Add a final 110 ml/½ cup cold water, bring up the heat slightly and cook for another 20 minutes. The lentils should be evenly cooked, soft and the texture should be like a thick mash. Slice the kombu thinly and put back into the lentils. Discard the bay leaf.

While the lentils are cooking, wash the aubergines/eggplants lengthways and chop them into 3-mm/⅛-in. slices. Place in a large sieve/strainer or a bowl and sprinkle ½ teaspoon of the salt over the slices. Massage it in and let them sit for at least 15 minutes. Pat dry with paper towels. Peel the potatoes and slice them lengthways into 2-mm/⅛-in. slices. Pat these dry as well.

Heat 1 tablespoon of the oil in a large frying pan/skillet and heat over a medium heat. Add one batch of aubergine/eggplant, wait until the flesh starts browning, then turn. It soaks up a lot of oil, but don't add more than 1 tablespoon per batch, if you can help it. Repeat with the remaining slices, adding new oil for each batch. Add the rest of the oil to the pan (it should generously cover the bottom) and fry the potato slices in 3 batches, just until golden on both sides. Then, season them with the remaining ½ teaspoon salt.

Preheat the oven to 180°C (350°F) Gas 4. Cover the bottom of the oiled baking pan with fried potato slices. Add half of the lentils and spread evenly. Layer the aubergine/eggplant slices and spread over the tomato sauce, then add another layer of aubergine, and some potatoes, if any left. Cover it all with the remaining lentils.

To prepare the béchamel sauce, place the oil in the frying pan, add the flour and whisk continuously for a couple of minutes over a medium heat until golden brown and fragrant, then add the milk little by little, and continue stirring until the sauce boils. It should turn out like a creamy, thick sauce without any lumps. Add the white miso (not essential but it adds a nice aroma and sweetness), salt, nutmeg and pepper to taste. Whisk once more and remove from heat. Pour the sauce over the lentils, spreading it evenly with a spatula. Bake for about 40 minutes or until well browned.

# soft-shell veggie tacos

I've never bought pre-made tortillas; one glance at the ingredients makes me want to look for organic cornmeal instead! And when I fill homemade tortillas with a nice, spicy filling and take a bite, I understand why so many people prefer tacos to sandwiches!

**For the tortillas**

260 g/2 cups fine cornmeal

130 g/1 cup spelt flour or unbleached plain/ all-purpose flour, plus extra for kneading

1 teaspoon sea salt

1 teaspoon active dry yeast (additive-free)

3 tablespoons sunflower oil

230 ml/1 cup lukewarm water

**For the filling**

320 g/1¾ cups cooked kidney beans

4 tablespoons olive oil

1 large onion, diced

4 garlic cloves, crushed

¼ teaspoon sea salt

1 medium red (bell) pepper, diced

1 teaspoon ground cumin

¼ teaspoon chilli powder, or to taste

1 teaspoon dried oregano

2 tablespoons soy sauce

1 tablespoon apple cider vinegar

1 tablespoon rice or agave syrup

200 g/1 cup organic canned corn kernels, drained

2 tablespoons water

30 g/½ cup chopped mixed spring onion/scallion and coriander/cilantro

Serves 2-4

To make the tortillas, mix all the dry ingredients well in a large bowl, then incorporate the oil. Add enough of the water to get a slightly softer ball of dough. Flour a clean work surface and knead the dough for a couple of minutes, adding flour when needed but keeping the dough soft. Form 2 cylinders out of the dough, cover with a tea/dish towel and let sit in the oven with only the light on (no heat) for at least 15 minutes. Take them out and cut each cylinder into 4–5 equal pieces. With a rolling pin, roll out each tortilla to the size of a small dessert plate, and not too thin. Sprinkle with flour to avoid sticking. Remember not to place rolled tortillas on top of each other! Place the raw tortilla on a pre-heated cast-iron or stainless-steel frying pan/skillet and allow to cook for about 30 seconds until it begins to puff up with air pockets, then turn and cook for another 30 seconds. Keep the done tortillas covered with a tea/dish towel to keep them warm and from drying out.

Meanwhile, to make the filling, use a fork to crush 140 g/¾ cup cooked kidney beans to get a chunky mash. Set aside. Heat the oil in a frying pan and sauté onion and garlic with the salt until translucent, then add the diced red (bell) pepper, cumin, chilli powder and oregano and continue to sauté for 10 more minutes, stirring occasionally. Add the soy sauce, vinegar and syrup and bring to a boil. Add the corn, along with the crushed and remaining whole kidney beans and the water, and combine well over a medium heat.

Now, sprinkle over the chopped spring onion/scallion and coriander/cilantro and then taste the filling, adjusting the seasoning if necessary.

Serve the warm tortillas with the filling evenly divided over them (it should be enough for 6–8 tortillas). Any type of lightly seasoned salad adds freshness to this dish, but I sometimes serve them garnished with Avocado Pasta Sauce (page 107) or Strong-flavoured Tomato Sauce (page 99).

# polenta tarte flambée

There is at least one recipe with polenta in all my cookbooks, and this book won't be an exception! Visually appealing and a song for your taste buds, this dish is crispy and full of summer flavours. The look and texture reminded me of the tarte flambée that I first tried in a small beach restaurant on a German island in the middle of the North Sea. This is my gluten-free and vegan version that I hope you will enjoy!

750 ml/3 cups water

160 g/1 cup polenta

100 g/1 cup grated courgette/zucchini

50 g/⅓ cup finely diced onion

70 g /½ cup finely grated smoked tofu

2–3 firm tomatoes

olive oil for sprinkling and serving

½ teaspoon dried basil

sea salt and crushed black pepper

fresh basil, to garnish

35-cm x 25-cm/14–in. x 10–in. casserole dish or baking pan, well-oiled

**Serves 2–3**

Preheat the oven to 200°C (400°F) Gas 6. Bring the water to a boil, add ½ teaspoon sea salt and whisk in the polenta. Lower the heat, cover and let cook for 15 minutes. There's no need to stir. Lightly salt the grated courgette/zucchini, let sit for 5 minutes and then squeeze out as much of the water as you can. Add the onion, courgette/zucchini and grated smoked tofu to the cooked polenta and mix well. Add salt and pepper to taste. Spoon the polenta mix into the oiled casserole dish or baking pan, evening the surface with a spatula or wet hands. Slice the tomatoes into 5-mm/⅕-in. thick slices and discard any excess juice and seeds. Arrange the tomato slices in a single layer over the top and sprinkle with olive oil, salt, dried basil and crushed black pepper to taste. Bake for 20–25 minutes or until golden brown and until the tomatoes are well baked and sizzling. Let it cool a little, and then slice and serve with fresh basil, a generous splash of olive oil and some Strong-flavoured Tomato Sauce (page 99) or Mock Tomato Sauce (page 100) to make this dish more juicy.

You can make variations on this recipe, topping the polenta with thin slices of courgette/zucchini, (bell) peppers or aubergine/eggplant instead of tomatoes. Bon appétit!

# versatile vegan pizzas

By combining two types of pizza dough, two types of red sauce and two types of vegan 'cheese', you can get 8 different kinds of pizza! Also, add on top things like olives, onion slices, mushrooms, etc., sprinkle with dried oregano, bake and enjoy! Apart from the Nut Cheese recipe on pages 16-17, here is a recipe for a tangy tofu and rice mix that, by adding the right amount of spices, has a nice texture and the taste of cream cheese.

1 portion Basic Yeast Dough or Basic Yeast-free Pizza Dough (page 24)

½ portion Strong-flavoured Tomato Sauce (page 99)

vegetables of your choosing (olives, sliced onion, sliced mushrooms, etc.) for topping

1 tablespoon olive oil

1 teaspoon dried oregano

### For the tofu cream cheese

150 g/¾ cup cooked brown rice (page 15)

200 g/6½ oz. fresh soft tofu

60 g/½ cup finely diced onion

4 tablespoons olive oil

1 tablespoon umeboshi vinegar or 2 teaspoons umeboshi paste

sea salt, to taste

40-cm x 32-cm/16-in. x 12½-in. baking pan, well-oiled

Makes one 27-cm/10½-in. diameter pizza

To make the tofu cream cheese, blend the rice, tofu, onion, oil and vinegar or paste in a food processor or blender until smooth. Depending on how soft your tofu is, you might need to add water little by little, to achieve a consistency of thick cream cheese. Add salt (umeboshi vinegar/paste is salty, so be careful not to add too much). This cheese is even better if left to rest in the fridge for 24 hours. Try adding dark sesame oil or tahini instead of olive oil, for a slightly different aroma.

Follow the instructions for making and rolling out the pizza dough on page 24. Once you have transferred your pizza base to the baking pan, spread with the tomato sauce, then top with spoonfuls of the tofu cream cheese (or use the Nut Cheese on pages 16–17) and vegetables of your choosing and sprinkle with olive oil and oregano. Bake as instructed on page 24.

I find that baking the pizza on the bottom surface of the oven is the best way to do it, since baking the pizza for too long in the middle of the oven makes the dough hard and overly crispy.

# appetizers, snacks & lunchboxes

# vegan sushi

There's no reason to think of sushi as a complicated Japanese delicacy that you can't make at home. So here are my instructions to make two types of sushi: maki, where the nori is on the outside of the roll, and California rolls, where the nori is on the inside.

### For the spread

65 g/½ cup dry-roasted sunflower seeds (or use 4 tablespoons tahini)

3 teaspoons umeboshi paste

1 tablespoon dark sesame oil

### For the sushi

2 medium pickled gherkins, cut lengthways into strips, or other pickled vegetables (sauerkraut, daikon, etc.)

1 long carrot, cut lengthways into thin sticks

4 long spring onion/scallion leaves, washed and drained

4 toasted nori sheets

475 g/2⅔ cups cooked brown rice (page 15)

1 long carrot, cut lengthways into thin sticks

### For the dipping sauce

2 tablespoons fresh ginger juice

2 teaspoons tamari

2 tablespoons dry-roasted sesame seeds

4 tablespoons water

extra pickles and wasabi paste, to serve

a sushi mat

### Makes 32 pieces

Prepare the spread by blending the sunflower seeds in a blender into a powder/butter, and then adding the umeboshi and oil. The spread is very salty and not meant to be eaten on its own!

Prepare a bowl full of lukewarm water to wet your hands with while making the sushi. Place each nori sheet in turn on a sushi mat, shiny-side down. Wet your hands and spread 120 g/¾ cup of the cooked rice evenly over the nori, except the top side, where you'll want to leave a 1-cm/⅓-in. margin to make it easier to roll and seal.

To make the maki, spread a tablespoon of the spread across the middle of the roll. Place the gherkin strips, carrot sticks and spring onion/scallion leaves over the spread, making sure the layer is not thick, as this will make for an overly thick sushi.

Starting from the bottom, roll up the nori and tuck in the vegetables. Continue rolling and press tightly so that the rolled sushi stays sealed. Before serving, slice each sushi into 8 same-sized pieces. Repeat the whole process for the other 3 nori sheets, so you end up with 32 pieces of sushi.

To make California rolls, cover the sushi mat with a sheet of clingfilm/plastic wrap and place one nori sheet on top. Wet your hands and spread 120–150 g/¾–1 cup of the rice over the nori, distributing it evenly up to the edges. Carefully flip the nori so that the rice side goes on top of the clingfilm/plastic wrap on the mat. Spoon a tablespoon of the spread in a strip across the middle of the roll. Place the gherkin, carrot sticks and spring onion/scallion leaves over the spread. Starting at the edge while pressing it firmly, roll up the sushi mat and continue until you reach the end of the mat. Be careful not to wrap the clingfilm/plastic wrap inside! Squeeze the sushi inside the mat with your hands. Unwrap before serving, and slice each sushi into 8 same-sized pieces. Roll each of these pieces in toasted sesame seeds.

To make the sauce, mix the ginger juice, tamari and water. Dip a piece of sushi in it, then, before eating, coat it in some sesame seeds (but not for the California rolls, as they won't need it!)

Serve the sushi with extra pickles and, if you wish, a little wasabi paste, to spice things up!

# courgette & walnut canapés

Fresh, crunchy but also quite filling, these little canapés won't pass unnoticed! My grandma was shocked when I told her that courgette/zucchini can be eaten raw, since it's traditionally always cooked (and more often overcooked!). I'm sure that raw courgette/zucchini isn't something new for you, however, and that you'll enjoy making these canapés and offering them to your friends and family!

140 g/1 cup chopped walnuts

2 tablespoons chopped flat-leaf parsley

4 dried tomato halves, soaked, drained and chopped

½ teaspoon sweet paprika

⅛ teaspoon chilli powder

juice of ½ lemon

a little almond milk or water

1 medium courgette/zucchini, sliced diagonally into 3-mm/⅛-in. slices

30 g/½ cup alfalfa, chia and radish or other seed sprouts

sea salt, if necessary

Makes 20 canapés

Blend all the ingredients (except the liquid, initially, courgette/zucchini and the seed sprouts) in a food processor or blender into a thick paste, seasoning with salt to taste. You're looking for a dense consistency that will spread and safely stay on a courgette/zucchini slice, but add a little almond milk or water if it's too thick. Taste and add more seasoning, if needed.

Gently pat the courgette/zucchini slices with paper towels if they're moist. Top with 1–2 teaspoons of the spread and garnish with some seed sprouts. Continue until you use up all the courgette/zucchini slices. Serve immediately, since the saltiness of the spread might make the courgette/zucchini wilt and let out its moisture. Depending on how much spread you used for each canapé you might have some leftover. This spread will keep in the fridge for a couple of days, so don't worry.

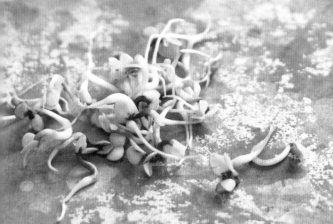

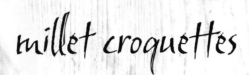

# millet croquettes

Leftover Millet Mash is great for making croquettes, so I always make more than we can eat in one go. I've added a little twist with a nori wrap.

1 portion Millet Mash (page 14)

1–2 nori sheets

vegetable oil, for deep-frying

Serves 2–4

Follow the recipe for Millet Mash on page 14. Let the mash cool completely, wet your hands and form 6-cm/2½-in. wide croquettes. Don't worry if they are a little soft, as the crust will form during frying. Cut the nori sheets into 10-cm x 1-cm/4-in. x ⅓-in. strips and wrap loosely around the middle of each croquette, wetting the end of the strip with a drop of water to seal. Deep-fry them in hot oil (do not cram the pan!) and drain on paper towels before serving. These croquettes can be served as appetizers, as a side dish (instead of a plain grain) or instead of croutons in soups and salads.

# potato mash & vegan gnocchi

Eggs are really redundant in the gnocchi dough, and this recipe proves it. If you're in the mood for a more simple side dish, just make the first part of the recipe - creamy mash!

470 g/16½ oz./3 large potatoes

80 ml/⅓ cup non-dairy milk

2 tablespoons non-hydrogenated margarine

¾ teaspoon salt

a pinch each of ground nutmeg and crushed black pepper

145 g /1 cup plus 2 tablespoons unbleached plain/all-purpose flour (if making gnocchi)

sea salt

Serves 2–3

Peel and wash the potatoes. Cut them into wedges and cover with water in a saucepan. Let boil, lower the heat and cook for 15 minutes or until soft. Drain and let cool slightly. Mash with a potato masher. Heat the milk and margarine until the margarine melts. Add the salt, nutmeg and pepper to the potatoes and stir in the milk mixture. The mash is ready and can be served as it is.

A more interesting way to use the mash is to make gnocchi. Add to the mash half of the flour and mix it in to get a very soft dough. Place it on a smooth, floured work surface and add the remaining flour little by little until you get a smooth dough that doesn't stick to your hands.

Form 3 cylinders about 3 cm/1¼ in. thick, place on a floured tray and refrigerate for 30 minutes, or longer. Boil a saucepan of water with a little salt. Take the dough out of the fridge and cut each cylinder into small gnocchi, 3 cm/1¼ in. long. Add to the pan and cook for 3–5 minutes until the gnocchi start coming up to the surface and the middle isn't soggy. Drain and serve them immediately drizzled with olive oil, fried garlic slices, crushed black pepper and sage leaves.

# cherry tomatoes filled with spinach pesto

*These small, delicate bites are a real treat not only because of their fresh taste but also because the bright red and light green combination of colours really gets noticed! They can be served not only as appetizers but also as amuse-bouche, to impress your guests.*

20 cherry tomatoes

2 handfuls of baby spinach

85 g/⅔ cup sunflower seeds

4 tablespoons olive oil

2 garlic cloves, peeled

1 teaspoon lemon juice (to prevent oxidation of greens)

1–2 tablespoons of water, if necessary

sea salt

*Makes 20*

Wash the tomatoes and remove their stems. Next, cut a very thin layer off the bottom of each tomato so that they can sit on a serving plate without rolling. Slice off the tops and scoop out the flesh with a small spoon to make enough space for the filling. Do this carefully so as not to damage the tomatoes.

Wash and drain the spinach well. Lightly dry-roast the sunflower seeds to release their full aroma. Place all the ingredients (except the tomatoes) in a blender and blend until smooth. Add the water if necessary; the pesto should be liquid enough to be easily spooned or piped into the cored cherry tomatoes.

Fill each tomato carefully and serve immediately on fresh lettuce and seed sprouts, if desired.

If in season, use wild garlic (bear's garlic) instead of spinach for a beautiful aroma and an even more fluorescent green colour! Other soft greens and herbs work well, too. Also, you can use almonds, pine nuts, hazelnuts, sesame seeds, cashews and any other nuts and seeds instead of sunflower seeds to make this pesto.

# buckwheat crackers

Buckwheat is a really healthy seed that is often overlooked, but I think it's a big shame not to eat it from time to time! Try these crackers as a snack topped with chutney (page 108) or roasted vegetables.

95 g /½ cup buckwheat

85 g/⅔ cup sunflower seeds

100 g/1 cup grated vegetables or leftover pulp

¾ teaspoon sea salt

1 medium red (bell) pepper, seeded

60 g/½ cup diced onion

½ teaspoon dried oregano

¼ teaspoon dried thyme

¼ teaspoon dried basil

2 tablespoons ground flaxseed

3 tablespoons olive oil

110 ml/½ cup vegetable juice or water

40-cm x 32-cm/16-in. x 12½-in. wire rack or baking pan

Makes 15

Preheat the oven to 80°C (175°F). In a high-speed blender, mix all the ingredients into a thick paste. Cut a piece of parchment paper to the size of your oven shelf/rack or baking pan and place it on a smooth surface. Spoon the paste so that it's about 3-mm/⅛-in. onto the parchment paper in a large rectangle. Put the oven rack/baking pan on the edge of your kitchen counter and quickly pull the parchment paper to slide it on. Place the oven shelf/rack or baking pan in the upper part of the oven; turn the heat up to 100°C (210°F), but prop the door open with a folded tea/dish towel, to ensure proper dehydration of the buckwheat. Dehydrate for 2–3 hours.

Peel off the parchment paper, and use a pizza cutter to cut the crackers into the desired shape; dehydrate the crackers directly on the oven shelf/rack for another 30 minutes if you want them really crispy. I love them a bit on the soft side, but dry crackers last longer without spoiling. Spoon on your chutney or roasted veggies to serve.

# seed falafel

Here's a fry-free and chickpea-free falafel that's surprisingly easy to make. It's also a great lunchbox item and the mix can stay fresh in the fridge for days. These green balls go with just about anything – in salads, with cooked vegetables, alongside soups or as an appetizer. It's a great way to introduce more seeds into your diet!

130 g/1 cup pumpkin seeds

130 g/1 cup sunflower seeds

50 g/½ cup walnuts

5 tablespoons chopped flat-leaf parsley

5 dried tomato halves, soaked

2 garlic cloves, crushed

3 tablespoons olive oil

juice of ½ a lemon

1 teaspoon dried oregano

1 tablespoon water, if necessary

sea salt and crushed black pepper, to taste

Makes 24

Grind the seeds in a food processor or blender into a fine flour, making sure you don't process them for too long, otherwise they might turn into seed butter. Finely chop the walnuts, as they'll give the falafels a nice crunchy texture. Add them, together with the remaining ingredients, (except the water) to the seed flour and mix well with your hands or with a silicone spatula. Taste and adjust the seasoning if necessary – it should taste strong and full of flavour. Try squeezing the seed mixture in your hand and if it doesn't fall apart it's moist enough. In case it feels dry and crumbles immediately, add the water and mix again.

Form the mixture into walnut-sized falafel balls and either serve them up or keep them refrigerated before use. I find that it's always a good idea to keep a stash of these falafels in the fridge!

# salads

# wild rice with rocket & pine nuts

Wild rice has a wonderful taste and texture – it's a type of grass native to the Great Lakes region of North America. High in protein, fibre, minerals and vitamins, wild rice should have its place in your weekly menu. And when mixed as I show you below, it'll be delicious, too!

250 ml/1 cup water

110 g/⅔ cup wild rice

a pinch of sea salt

60 g/½ cup black olives, pitted and chopped

70 g/½ cup lightly toasted pine nuts or other nuts/seeds

4 handfuls of rocket/arugula, baby spinach or any other soft greens

### For the Mediterranean vinaigrette

60 g/⅓ cup extra virgin olive oil

balsamic or apple cider vinegar, to taste

a handful of basil leaves, finely chopped

1 garlic clove, crushed

4 tablespoons water

sea salt and crushed black pepper

Serves 1–2

In a saucepan, bring the water to a boil and add the rice and salt, then reduce the heat, cover and cook for about 25 minutes or until the rice is soft and the water is completely absorbed. If wild rice isn't available, then you can use any other non-sticky cooked whole grains and add them to the olives and pine nuts.

For the vinaigrette, place all the ingredients in a jar, close and shake. In a large salad bowl, mix the cooked rice, olives and pine nuts. Add the vinaigrette and mix well. Wash and drain the greens, then add to the salad just before serving.

# salad Olivier

This is my vegan version of a very popular festive dish served in many countries, and in Croatia we incorrectly call it Franscuska salata (French salad). I serve it as a side dish to baked vegetables and/or tofu, tempeh, steamed veggies or fried foods. With some crackers or flatbread, it can easily serve as a satisfying light lunch or dinner.

2 medium potatoes

750 ml/3 cups water

150 g/1 cup peas, fresh or frozen

3 small carrots, diced

70g /½ cup diced pickles

200 g/scant cup of Tofu Mayonnaise or Sunflower Seed & Cashew Mayonnaise (page 103)

Serves 2-3

In a saucepan, cover the potatoes with cold water and let them boil, uncovered. Lower the heat and cook them until soft, but not overcooked – about 20–25 minutes. Drain and let them cool, and then peel and dice before setting them aside.

In a medium-sized saucepan bring the water to a boil, add the peas and cook them until soft but still bright green. To save time, place a steamer basket or a fitting colander on top or the pan while the peas are still cooking and steam the diced carrots, covered, until they're soft. Drain the peas and leave the vegetables to cool.

In a large salad bowl, combine the peas, carrots, potatoes and diced pickles. Pour over the mayonnaise and mix well to cover all the vegetables. Taste and add seasoning if necessary; since the mayo recipe isn't overly strong, you might need to add more salt, pepper, vinegar or oil, according to taste.

# pink quinoa salad with fennel & arame

*Having a plate full of lively colours every day of the week keeps you healthy inside out! Even if you don't really like raw beet(root), I'm using only a small amount here that can barely be tasted but gives an amazingly vibrant pink colour to this salad!*

850 ml/3¾ cups water

170 g/1 cup quinoa

130 g/1⅓ cups thinly sliced fennel bulb

3 tablespoons lemon juice

20 g/1 cup dried arame strips

1 teaspoon tamari

½ small beet(root), finely grated

1 tablespoon umeboshi vinegar

3 tablespoons sesame oil

3 spring onions/scallions, finely chopped

2 tablespoons dry-roasted sunflower seeds (optional)

sea salt

**Serves 2**

In a saucepan, bring 400 ml/1¾ cups of the water to a boil. Wash the quinoa, drain it well and add it to the boiling water together with ¼ teaspoon salt. Lower the heat, cover and let simmer for 20 minutes or until the water is completely absorbed and then turn off the heat.

Place the sliced fennel in a bowl, add 2 tablespoons of the lemon juice and ½ teaspoon salt and squeeze well with your hands, until the fennel starts 'sweating'.

To cook the arame, put the strips in a small saucepan, add the remaining water and let boil, uncovered. Lower the heat, half-cover and cook for 15 minutes. Drain off the excess water, add the tamari and quickly stir over a low heat until it is absorbed.

In a large salad bowl, mix the grated beet(root) with the vinegar, which helps to accentuate the bright pink colour. Add the cooked quinoa, the remaining lemon juice, 4 tablespoons cooked arame and the oil. Just before serving, mix in the fennel and spring onions/scallions. Taste and season with some more salt and lemon juice if necessary. To add extra texture to this salad, sprinkle the dry-roasted sunflower seeds over it.

# home-fermented kimchi

This is just one of many variations of kimchi. Pickling at home is often neglected and people do not realise how important it is for good digestion to eat naturally fermented foods on a daily basis. You can always have a couple of jars in different stages of fermentation in your pantry and take a spoonful or two every day with your main meal – it's that easy! It's worth making plenty at once and using it up in 30–60 days.

1.2 litres/5 cups water

3 tablespoons sea salt

600 g/7 cups julienned green cabbage

180 g/2½ cups leeks, chopped

10 g/1 handful of dulse seaweed

20 g/¾ oz. piece of fresh ginger, peeled

4 garlic cloves, peeled

1 teaspoon ground turmeric

1 whole medium-sized chilli/chile pepper

*pickle press, optional*

Makes 12–15 servings

Make a brine by mixing the water and salt and stirring well until the salt dissolves. Put the cabbage and leeks into a pickle press and cover with the brine. To keep them submerged, screw the lid down just a little. Allow to soak for a few hours, or overnight if possible. If you don't have a pickle press, put the vegetables in a bowl and weigh them down by resting a plate on top of them.

In the meantime, crush the ginger and garlic. Soak the dulse seaweed in cold water for 30 minutes, drain and finely chop.

Drain the soaked vegetables, but be sure to keep the brine. Mix the turmeric in with the vegetables, seaweed, crushed ginger and garlic and add the chilli/chile pepper.

Put this mixture back into the pickle press or bowl and add enough brine to rise over the veggies once you press them down. Screw the lid down as much as you can, or, if using a plate, put something heavy on top of it. Allow to ferment for a minimum of a week. The best taste develops after 4 weeks!

# vegan Caesar salad

Don't be fooled by the fact that this is a salad – it really is a filling meal by itself!
Feel free to use different vegetables, but keep the mayo dressing and bread
croutons – this rounds up the salad and makes it delightfully rich.

### For the salad

6–8 leaves of Tuscan kale or
young kale

¼ teaspoon sea salt

juice of 1 lemon

250 g/9 oz. lettuce mix
(depending on the season you
can mix up to 3 varieties – oak
leaf, red leaf, rocket/arugula,
endive, romaine, watercress,
radicchio, lamb's lettuce/corn
salad, etc.)

½ ripe avocado

1 medium carrot (or other
root), finely grated

5 tablespoons alfalfa, garlic,
leek, cress or other seed
sprouts

4 tablespoons chopped
walnuts

100 g/1 cup croutons
(page 116)

10 chive flowers or other
edible flowers (optional)

### For the dressing

450g/ 2 cups Tofu Mayonnaise
or Sunflower Seed & Cashew
Mayonnaise (page 103)

Serves 2 as a main,
4 as a side

Wash and drain the kale leaves and then remove the stem
that runs up through the centre of each leaf. Slice the kale
thinly, sprinkle with the salt and lemon juice and massage
the leaves quickly before letting them marinate for 10 minutes.
This will soften them and make them easier to digest and
chew. Wash, drain and tear the lettuce leaves, and peel and
cube the avocado. In a large salad bowl, combine the lettuce,
avocado, grated carrot (or other root), seed sprouts, walnuts,
croutons and flowers (if using).

Pour over the chosen mayonnaise and, with the help of two
salad spoons, mix well until completely incorporated. Taste
and adjust the seasoning, adding more salt, vinegar or spices
of choice, if necessary. Let rest for 10 minutes before serving,
to allow the flavours to develop.

# pearled spelt salad with button mushrooms & watercress

Many people are avoiding wheat berries and choosing to use spelt and spelt products instead, since spelt is easier to digest and causes fewer allergic reactions. It has a nice chewy texture, both whole grain and pearled. Using pearled is less time-consuming, as it cooks in 20 minutes, but if you prefer using whole grain, you can (follow the method on page 15). Combined with a refreshing dressing, it makes for a light and nutritious lunch.

440 ml/2 cups water

190 g/1 cup pearled spelt, washed and drained

¼ teaspoon sea salt

150 g/2 cups sliced button mushrooms

3 teaspoons tamari

1 teaspoon lemon juice

1 teaspoon sesame oil

### For the dressing
2 handfuls of watercress, washed and drained

¼ teaspoon sea salt, or to taste

2 tablespoons chopped hazelnuts

2 tablespoons olive oil

2 tablespoons lemon juice

3 tablespoons chopped dry-roasted hazelnuts, to garnish

*Serves 2*

In a saucepan, bring the water to a boil, then add the spelt and the salt, lower the heat to a minimum and cover. Cook for 20 minutes or until the spelt is chewy but soft. Drain any liquid that remains, if any, and allow the spelt to cool slightly.

Coat the mushrooms in the tamari and lemon juice. Heat the oil in a heavy-bottomed frying pan/skillet, then add the mushrooms and fry for only 1–2 minutes until they start wilting slightly. Turn off the heat, transfer the mushrooms to a bowl and let cool.

To prepare the green dressing, place all the ingredients, except a couple of watercress sprigs to garnish the dish at the end, in a blender jug and blend until smooth and creamy. Taste and adjust the seasoning, if necessary. The dressing should be slightly salty to enhance the flavour of the cooked spelt.

When ready to serve, combine the spelt and mushrooms and top with 2 full tablespoons of the dressing. Sprinkle with the chopped nuts and add the watercress sprigs. Let each person mix in the dressing just before eating, otherwise it might look a bit messy on the plate!

# sauces & dips

# strong-flavoured tomato sauce

Buying ready-made sauces has never been my thing. Making stuff from scratch is so satisfying and the taste of homemade foods really makes a difference. I'm lucky to have my own garden where we grow juicy tomatoes, pick them at their peak, make passata/strained tomatoes and can it for later use. If you don't have your own passata, use organic passata or peeled canned tomatoes for a chunkier texture. It's really important to have premium-quality tomatoes to make this divine tomato sauce!

1 portion Soffritto (page 19)

3 dried tomato halves, soaked, drained and chopped

1 teaspoon vegetable bouillon powder or ½ bouillon cube (not essential)

½ teaspoon dried oregano

½ teaspoon dried basil

1 tablespoon rice, agave or maple syrup

1 tablespoon tamari

¼ teaspoon sea salt

crushed black pepper

570 ml /2½ cups passata/strained tomatoes

3 garlic cloves, crushed

2 tablespoons chopped parsley or chives

olive oil, to finish

*Makes 650 ml /2¾ cups*

When the soffritto vegetables are tender, add the dried tomatoes, bouillon, dried herbs, syrup, tamari and salt and pepper to taste and stir until vegetables soak up the spices, for about two minutes. Next, add the passata, bring up the heat and let boil. Now lower the heat and leave to simmer, uncovered, for about 10 minutes, depending on how thick you want your sauce to be.

At the very end, add the garlic, parsley or chives and an extra drop of olive oil.

Use for pasta, pizza and, in small quantities, to add flavour to stews, ragouts and soups. If you have leftovers, use within 3 days or freeze for later use.

# mock tomato sauce

Why mock when you can have the real thing, you might wonder? Two reasons, really. Firstly, tomatoes are omnipresent and it's nice to mix things up a bit. Secondly, this is a great way of feeding your family with an array of vegetables without them noticing, because this will fool even the pickiest eaters out there! Use carrots when pumpkins are out of season or use both if you can.

470 g/17 oz. pumpkin, peeled and seeded

1 medium beet(root), peeled

1 medium onion, peeled

2 bay leaves

470 ml/2 cups water

3 garlic cloves, crushed

3 tablespoons olive oil

½ teaspoon dried oregano

¼ teaspoon crushed black pepper

1 tablespoon umeboshi vinegar or ½ tablespoon apple cider vinegar

sea salt

pressure cooker, optional

Makes 650 ml/2¾ cups

Cut the pumpkin into 5-cm/2-in. chunks, chop the beet(root) into thin slices and cut the onion into 2-cm/¾-in. chunks. Place all the vegetables in a pressure cooker, add the bay leaves, water and ¼ teaspoon salt and follow the manufacturer's instructions to bring to high pressure, then pressure cook for about 20 minutes until all the vegetables are very soft. Alternatively, use a heavy-bottomed pot, put on a medium-high heat, cover and bring to the boil, then lower the heat and cook for around 30 minutes. To check if they're done, prick the pumpkin and beet(root) with a fork – if there's no resistance, they're ready!

Now take most of the beet(root) slices out as well as half of the cooking liquid (save it for later). Next, blend the vegetables in a food processor or blender briefly, which will produce a thick, orangey mixture. Start adding the remaining beet(root) and some of the liquid little by little, and blend until you reach the bright red tomato colour and the consistency of a sauce.

To finish the sauce, add the garlic, olive oil, oregano, pepper, and the umeboshi vinegar or apple cider vinegar, which will make the sauce taste 'tomatoey'. Season to taste with salt.

If you did everything by the book, you will have a batch of mock tomato sauce. Well done! Use it on pizza, as pasta sauce or dilute it and serve as everyone's favourite 'tomato' soup!

# tofu mayonnaise

We all know that the 'normal' mayonnaise is really unhealthy. Also, there are many vegan substitutes on the market that are almost equally unhealthy, with high levels of saturated fats and additives. Once you start making these healthy vegan mayonnaises, you won't look back. I haven't met a person who didn't like them!

300 g/10 oz. fresh tofu

6 tablespoons water

4 tablespoons olive or sunflower oil

3 tablespoons lemon juice or apple cider vinegar

1 soft date

½ teaspoon sea salt

Makes 350 g/1½ cups

Blend all the ingredients in a blender until the mixture is completely smooth. Taste and adjust the seasonings. I like it more tangy than sweet, so I always add a little more lemon juice or vinegar. Also, pay attention to what you will serve it with. If you use it as a salad dressing, it needs to be a little bit more sour, so add a little more lemon juice or vinegar; if used with salty foods like burgers or chips, make it less salty.

# sunflower & cashew mayonnaise

85 g/⅔ cup sunflower seeds

95 g/⅔ cup cashews

3 tablespoons olive oil

¾ teaspoon sea salt

4 tablespoons lemon juice

1 soft date

200 ml/¾ cup cold water

1 tablespoon apple cider vinegar

2 garlic cloves, peeled (optional)

Makes 400 g/1⅔ cups

Soak the seeds and nuts in cold water overnight, then drain, discarding the liquid, rinse and drain again. Add them to the blender with all the other ingredients and blend until completely smooth. For the best results, use a high-speed blender to achieve a lovely velvety consistency.

For serving, follow the instructions for Tofu Mayonnaise above so that you don't make it too bland or too salty.

# onion gravy

*A quick and simple recipe to make when you feel you need to juice up your meal!
I use this gravy over Millet Mash (page 14), among other recipes!*

4 tablespoons light sesame oil

a pinch of sea salt

90 g/¾ cup onion, sliced into thin half-moons

4 garlic cloves (optional)

1 tablespoon soy sauce

1 teaspoon apple cider vinegar

1 teaspoon rice or agave syrup

2 tablespoons unbleached plain/all-purpose flour

250 ml/1 cup water

2 teaspoons Dijon mustard

crushed black pepper

2 tablespoons chopped herbs

*Makes 500 ml/2 cups*

Slice the onions in thin half-moons lengthways. Add the sesame oil and salt to a large frying pan/skillet over a low heat and sauté the onions until they're translucent and soft. You can also add a few chopped fresh mushrooms or 2 tablespoons soaked, drained and chopped dried mushrooms to the onions while sautéeing, for extra flavour. Add 4 crushed garlic cloves if desired, and cook until fragrant. Slightly bring up the heat, add the soy sauce, vinegar and syrup and stir well until it sizzles.

Slowly add the flour and whisk vigorously for a minute, then, still whisking, add the water little-by-little until a gravy consistency is reached. There should be no flour lumps! (If you want to avoid flour you can use a diluted thickener of choice, such as cornflour/cornstarch, kuzu or arrowroot powder). Add mustard and pepper, taste and add more soy sauce if needed. Finally, sprinkle with chopped herbs to garnish, just before serving.

# stir-fry sauce

*I make this sauce weekly, since my husband is such a fan of stir-fries! It is also a
great way to sneak in many vegetables that he wouldn't be happy to eat otherwise!*

2 tablespoons crushed ginger

½ teaspoon ground ginger

2 tablespoons crushed garlic

3 tablespoons soy sauce

2 tablespoons toasted sesame oil

1 tablespoon rice or agave syrup

⅛ teaspoon chilli/chile powder

1 teaspoon lemon juice

about 100 ml/⅓ cup water

2 tablespoons sesame seeds

3 tablespoons sliced spring onion/scallion

*Makes 150 ml/⅔ cup*

Blend all the ingredients (except the sesame seeds and spring onion/scallion, which you'll add just before serving) in a food processor or blender until the mixture is fairly smooth.

I use this sauce to marinate tofu, seitan or tempeh prior to stir-frying them with vegetables, before adding noodles and then pouring the leftover sauce in the wok until absorbed. I also use it to serve with Vegan Sushi (page 71), or as a dip for Millet Croquettes (page 75) or Spicy Burgers (page 54).

# avocado pasta sauce

*In my case, any dish with avocado is delicious! Apart from using it for guacamole, slicing it in salads or adding it to salsas, avocado can be blended up in a nice creamy sauce that goes amazingly well with a good-quality spelt or rice spaghetti. It will only take a couple of minutes to prepare and make you happy for much longer!*

1 ripe avocado

4 tablespoons olive oil

2 tablespoons umeboshi vinegar (or use soy sauce instead, or sea salt to taste)

2 tablespoons tahini

200 g/7 oz. dried spaghetti, cooked al dente and drained

handful of garlic sprouts, or other seed sprouts

2 tablespoons toasted black sesame seeds, to garnish

**Serves 2**

Peel and stone/pit the avocado, then blend along with the olive oil and umeboshi vinegar (or soy sauce or salt) in a food processor or a blender until smooth. Add a little water if it's very thick. Taste and adjust the seasoning, bearing in mind that it should be on the saltier side, since the pasta needs a strong sauce.

Pour the sauce over the hot pasta and mix thoroughly. Serve immediately, sprinkling each portion with half of the garlic (or other sprouts) and a tablespoon of black sesame seeds, to garnish.

You can use any nut or seed butter instead of tahini; peanut butter, for example, makes a nice sauce, too! You can basically make endless variations on this sauce, adding garlic, onion, lemon juice or crushed black pepper, all depending on what you have in your fridge or pantry. Bon appétit!

# roasted red pepper dip

*The best variety of peppers to use for this dip are red, long and pointed Romano peppers, but if you can't find them, use regular red (bell) peppers. Roasting peppers deepens their flavour and gives a wonderful aroma to this dip.*

1 kg/2¼ lb. Romano peppers

150 g/¾ cup olive oil

4 garlic cloves, crushed

1 tablespoon apple cider vinegar

sea salt

*Makes 230 g/1 cup*

Preheat the oven to 180°C (350°F) Gas 4. Wash and pat the peppers dry leaving them whole. Line a shallow baking pan with parchment paper and lay all the peppers next to each other in the pan. Turn the peppers frequently until the entire skin has become black and blistery. Remove from the oven and place them in an airtight container, tightly covered, for long enough to build up the steam, about 15 minutes. Make sure you save all the liquid that leaks from the peppers while cooling. Next, peel and seed the peppers, again saving any liquid. Cut the pepper flesh into small pieces. Heat the oil in a pan, add the peppers and garlic and fry for a couple of minutes with a pinch of salt. Add the vinegar, collected pepper juice and more salt and sauté over a medium heat for another 20 minutes or until the juice has been absorbed and the desired thickness is reached. Serve as a spread, or blend well, adding a little hot water or more oil, and serve as a dip.

# aubergine & date chutney

*This thick and slightly oily sauce bursts with flavours and makes a great condiment. I love serving it on toasted home-baked bread (page 27) or crackers (page 79).*

70 g/½ cup soft dates

2 large aubergines/eggplants

100 g/½ cup olive oil

240 g /2 cups onions, cut into thin half-moons

½ teaspoon fennel seeds

½ teaspoon cumin seeds

¼ teaspoon chilli powder

2 tablespoons tamari

2 tablespoons rice or apple cider vinegar

sea salt

*Makes 230 g/1 cup*

Soak the dates for at least one hour in warm water. Meanwhile, preheat the oven to 200°C (400°F) Gas 6. Wash the aubergines/eggplants and cut them in half lengthways. Oil the cut side a little and rub with ½ teaspoon salt. Prick the outer skin of all 4 halves with a fork. Lay them on a parchment-paper-lined baking sheet, cut side down. Bake for 40 minutes or until soft to the touch. Let them cool, peel off the skin and then dice the flesh.

Sauté the onions in the remaining oil with a pinch of salt over a low heat, stirring occasionally. Add the spices, cover and cook until caramelized, about 20 minutes. Drain and chop the dates, then add to the pan with the aubergine/eggplant, sautéeing for 5 more minutes. Add the tamari and vinegar, stir well and cook, uncovered, for another 5 minutes.

# soups & stews

# healing azuki bean stew with amaranth

*I can feel my body relaxing and my stomach thanking me while I'm eating this stew! It's made with only a couple of ingredients, the consistency is rich and creamy and the taste slightly sweet. After travelling, not eating well or a stressful day, this stew will take all your worries away!*

200 g/1 cup dried azuki beans

1 litre/4 cups cold water

180 g/1½ cups peeled, seeded and cubed Hokkaido or kabocha pumpkin

70 g/⅓ cup amaranth

2 tablespoons soy sauce

½ tablespoon umeboshi vinegar

½ teaspoon ground turmeric

½ teaspoon sea salt

*Serves 2–3*

Cover the azuki beans with the water in a saucepan and soak overnight (this is not necessary but will speed up the cooking). Bring them to a boil in the soaking water, then add the pumpkin and cook, half-covered, over a low heat until the azuki are half-done (about 30 minutes). Add the amaranth and cook until both the azuki and amaranth are soft (another 20–30 minutes). Season with the remaining ingredients and adjust the thickness by adding hot water, if necessary.

This stew doesn't have any oil and provides the body with a lot of well-balanced nutrients. It is a great winter dish when you feel exhausted and need comfort food that is easy to digest.

# creamy green soup

There's never enough green colour on our plates! I love to make a bright green nettle soup in nettle season (spring and autumn/fall), but other greens work well, too, like chard, spinach, young kale, wild garlic and broccoli. Avocado gives the soup its creaminess, but boiled potatoes, a few spoons of soy/soya, oat cream, or a teaspoon of diluted thickener can also be used.

1 litre/4 cups water

5 handfuls of green leafy vegetables (chard, spinach, kale, nettles, etc.)

¼ teaspoon sea salt

150 g/1 cup ripe avocado flesh

1 teaspoon lemon juice

1 tablespoon olive oil

1 tablespoon umeboshi vinegar

3 garlic cloves, crushed

1 serving of Gluten-free Croutons (page 27)

Serves 3

Bring the water to a boil in a large saucepan. Carefully wash the greens and drain off the excess water. If using kale, remove the hard stem running up the centre of each leaf. Add the greens to boiling water, cover and cook for 1–4 minutes, depending how soft the greens are – they should remain bright green in colour!

Add all the other ingredients and then transfer them into a food processor or a blender and blend until smooth. Taste and adjust the seasoning, if necessary.

Serve immediately with freshly-made Gluten-free Croutons (page 27).

# velvety red lentil soup

This is my favourite autumn/fall and winter soup! My clients might be a bit fed up with it, but since it is really very rich and yummy, I guess they forgive me for putting it on the menu almost every week during the pumpkin season. I hope you'll lick your plate, spoon, and saucepan, like I do every time I make it!

70 g/½ cup chopped leek (white part) or onion

4 tablespoons olive oil

a pinch of sea salt

200 g/1⅔ cups peeled and seeded pumpkin or squash wedges cut into 3–4-cm/1¼–1½-in. pieces

120 g/1 cup carrot cut into 2–3 cm/¼-1¼ in. pieces

1 teaspoon vegetable bouillon powder

¼ teaspoon ground turmeric

4 garlic cloves, crushed

2 bay leaves

3 dried tomato halves, chopped

2 tablespoons cooking wine

150 g/¾ cup dried red lentils, washed and drained

7-cm/ 2¾-in. strip of kombu seaweed

1 litre/4 cups water

a squeeze of lemon juice

a little crushed black pepper

1 tablespoon umeboshi vinegar

Serves 4

In a large saucepan, sauté the leek or onions in the olive oil with the salt, uncovered, until they're soft and transparent. Add the pumpkin or squash and carrot and sauté until the veggies start to 'sweat'. Add the bouillon powder, turmeric, garlic, bay leaves and tomatoes and stir. Next, pour in the wine and let the mixture boil. Now it's time to add the lentils, kombu and water. Turn up the heat, cover and bring to a boil. Then, lower the heat and let simmer for about 25–30 minutes or until the lentils and vegetables are completely tender (if pressure cooking, you'll only need to let it cook for 15 minutes).

At this point, remove the bay leaves. I usually use my handheld blender to purée the soup and make it creamy, but you can leave it as it is, if you like it chunky and more stew-like. Add the lemon juice, crushed pepper, and umeboshi vinegar and stir. Taste and add more spices if desired. You can add more hot water if the soup seems too thick, and it will definitely thicken as it cools.

Adding 80 g/⅔ cup diced beet(root) cubes together with the pumpkin and carrot will give this soup a nice earthy aroma and a lovely reddish-orange hue.

Leftovers are always welcome and this is one of the best things that could wait for me in the fridge after a hard day's work!

# Istrian minestrone

There is a 50 per cent chance that my grandma will serve this minestrone each time I visit her, and I always look forward to it! Many times she will use pasta that she freshly made that week instead of barley, but barley does make it chewy and more satisfying. The best season to make it is early summer, when peas are fresh from the pod and string beans are young and soft.

140 g/5 oz. yellow string beans or fresh corn kernels

4 tablespoons olive oil

1 large onion, diced

2 bay leaves

½ teaspoon fennel seeds

½ teaspoon dried basil

1 large carrot, diced

150 g/1 cup peas, fresh or frozen

1.2 litres/5 cups water

1½ tablespoons vegetable bouillon powder

110 g /½ cup cooked pearled barley, or 60 g/⅔ cup dried soup pasta (orzo, fidelini or ditalini)

30 g/1 cup fennel, spinach or other greens

2 garlic cloves, crushed

sea salt and crushed black pepper

Serves 4

Pinch off the tops of the string beans and cut the beans diagonally into 1.5-cm/½-in. pieces. Heat the oil in a large saucepan, add the onion, bay leaves, fennel seeds, dried basil and a pinch of salt and cook for a minute, then add the carrot and stir well. Cook for another minute or two, and repeat the same procedure with the peas and string beans or corn kernels, then stir everything together, cover and cook for about 10 minutes over a low to medium heat.

In another saucepan, bring the water to a boil and keep it warm.

Add the bouillon powder to the sautéed vegetables and stir well. Pour over the boiling water and bring to the boil again. Let cook for 10 minutes, and add the cooked pearled barley or dried pasta and let simmer for another 10 minutes. Add salt and pepper to taste. Chop the spinach (or other greens) and mix it with the crushed garlic in a small bowl. Add this to the minestrone a couple of minutes before serving. Serve with slices of Gluten-free Bread (page 27).

Serve this soup freshly cooked, especially if using pasta, since it soaks up a lot of the soup liquid when left to rest for too long, and you end up with a stew and not a soup!

This minestrone is a great way to use leftover pearled barley, but you can also cook it from scratch: follow the instructions for cooking brown rice (page 15) but use pearled barley instead of rice. Use some of the cooked barley to make the minestrone and save the rest for another dish in the coming days.

# kombu broth with tempura

A Japanese-style breakfast or lunch that will leave you feeling warm, relaxed and satisfied, and ready to continue with whatever you're doing. Serve in big bowls, sip the soup and use chopsticks to eat the noodles and veggies!

## For the soup

4 dried shiitake mushrooms

12-cm/4¾-in. strip of kombu seaweed

1.3 litres/5 cups water

2 small leeks

2 small carrots

2-cm/¾-in. piece of fresh ginger, crushed

3 garlic cloves

4 tablespoons dark sesame oil

tamari, to taste

2 tablespoons toasted sesame seeds

100 g/3½ oz. dried soba or udon noodles

## For the tempura

110 ml/½ cup ice-cold water

70 g /½ cup unbleached plain/all-purpose flour, refrigerated, plus extra for coating

¼ teaspoon ground turmeric

220 ml/1 scant cup sunflower oil, for frying

a selection of vegetables (courgette/zucchini, pumpkin, celeriac/celery root, sweet potato, onion, etc.), peeled and thinly sliced

sea salt

Serves 3–4

Place the shiitake and kombu in a saucepan and add water. Cover and let boil, then lower to a medium heat and let cook for 10 minutes. Remove the kombu and shiitake (slice the tops and discard stems), and keep the broth.

In a large saucepan, sauté the vegetables, ginger and garlic in the dark sesame oil for a couple of minutes. Add the sliced shiitake and the broth and let boil for 5–10 minutes. Season with plenty of tamari.

Cook the noodles separately until al dente, just before serving. If you cook them in the broth, they will soak up a lot of water and you'll end up with less soup than planned!

To make the batter, in a bowl, quickly mix the ice-cold water and flour with a whisk and add salt to taste and the turmeric. Do not over-mix – some lumps are alright. To make the tempura crispy, it's very important to use cold ingredients, not mix too much and use the batter for frying immediately.

Pat each vegetable slice dry with paper towels and roll into flour before dipping into the tempura so that he batter doesn't slide off. Heat the sunflower oil in a frying pan and when hot, dip a couple of vegetable pieces in the batter and fry until slightly golden. You will need about 4 pieces of veggies per person. If you feel the batter is too thin and doesn't stick properly to the floured vegetables, add a little more flour.

Drain the tempura vegetables on paper towels and serve immediately. Serve the cooked, drained noodles in the kombu broth sprinkled with the sesame seeds, with the tempura veggies on the side.

# hearty miso soup

Don't forget squashes and pumpkins! They're not only tasty and nourishing but also have a lot of beta-carotene – one of the most important antioxidants. However, the same applies to carrots, if you don't have a pumpkin at hand! This is a great soup to warm you up, at the same time feeding your body with vital enzymes from the miso paste.

2 tablespoons dark sesame oil

60 g/½ cup diced onion

60 g /½ cup peeled, seeded and cubed pumpkin, squash or carrots

4 garlic cloves, crushed

1 tablespoon crushed fresh ginger

800 ml/3½ cups cold water or bouillon (unsalted)

1 tablespoon barley or rice miso

¼ sheet toasted nori, cut into small pieces

1 tablespoon chopped flat-leaf parsley

1 teaspoon toasted sesame seeds

sea salt

Serves 2–3

In a large saucepan, sauté the onions for a minute or so in the sesame oil, before adding pumpkin, squash or carrot, along with the garlic, ginger and a pinch of salt. Sauté the mixture for a little longer, and then add the cold water or bouillon and cover. Bring to a boil, lower the heat and cook until the vegetables become tender.

Take 60 ml/¼ cup of the hot soup and put it in a small bowl. Now add the tablespoon of miso to it. Purée the miso really well with a fork, until it has completely melted. Put the miso liquid back into the soup. Taste and adjust the seasoning. Turn off the heat, cover and let the soup sit for a couple of minutes. Serve sprinkled with the pieces of nori, a sprinkling of sesame seeds, the chopped parsley and sesame seeds.

Don't forget that you can combine different kinds of miso in the same soup! Since hatcho (soya/soy bean) miso is of high quality but has a strong taste, try to combine ½ tablespoon soya/soy miso with ½ tablespoon barley miso, to get all the benefits of both kinds of soya/soy bean paste. In warmer weather, substitute darker miso pastes with sweet white miso, which is a lot milder.

# something sweet

# gooey chocolate cookies

Full of cocoa flavour and not overly sweet, these cookies will satisfy your chocolate craving the minute you bite into one! Make them a couple of times to see whether you prefer them soft and gooey or a little crispier.

60 g/2¼ oz. dark/bittersweet vegan chocolate, broken into pieces

65 g/⅓ cup sunflower oil

75 ml/⅓ cup soya/soy milk

200 g/¾ cup rice, maple or agave syrup

¼ teaspoon bourbon vanilla powder

130 g/1 cup unbleached plain/all-purpose flour

2 tablespoons cocoa powder

¾ teaspoon aluminium-free baking powder

¼ teaspoon sea salt

¼ teaspoon ground cinnamon

**Makes about 24 cookies**

Melt the chocolate in a heatproof bowl set over a pan of barely simmering water. Take care not to let the underside of the bowl touch the surface of the water. In a large mixing bowl, whisk the oil, milk, syrup and vanilla. Add the melted chocolate. Preheat the oven to 180°C (350°F) Gas 4. Place a sieve/strainer over the bowl containing the liquid ingredients (this way you won't need to use two separate bowls).

Put the flour, cocoa, cinnamon, baking powder and salt directly in the sieve/strainer and sift everything until it passes through the sieve/strainer net. Use a spatula to incorporate all the ingredients into a smooth batter. It should not slide down the spoon – if it does, chill the batter in the fridge for 10 minutes.

Line a baking sheet with parchment paper and, using a tablespoon, drop the batter onto it, 1 cm/⅓ in. apart. Bake for 12–14 minutes. The dough is dark to start with, so it's easy to burn them, and you want them still soft to the touch when you remove them from the oven. So check for doneness after 12 minutes, and bake them for no longer than 14 minutes.

Remove from the oven, slip the baking sheet with cookies onto the kitchen counter or a cold tray and let cool. Store in a cookie jar for a week or so.

# panna cotta

The Italian name panna cotta actually means 'cooked cream', and it's exactly that – cooked milk with cream thickened with gelatine. I'm, of course, using plant milk and cream as well as the amazing seaweed gelatine agar-agar. This is a very light, creamy and wobbly dessert – it takes only a couple of minutes to make it and some patience until it cools in the fridge!

220 ml/1 cup vanilla oat milk

220 ml/1 cup oat cream

1 heaped/heaping teaspoon agar-agar flakes

¼ teaspoon bourbon vanilla powder

70 g/¼ cup agave syrup

### For the sauce

3 tablespoons hazelnut butter

1 teaspoon cocoa powder

2 tablespoons agave syrup

a little Nut Milk (page 16) or water, if necessary

### Serves 3

In a saucepan, mix the oat milk and oat cream and add the agar-agar. Bring to the boil, then lower the heat and cook for 5 minutes or until the agar melts and you can't see any flakes left. Whisk in the vanilla powder and agave syrup and let the mixture boil again. Pour into dariole moulds or small ramekins and refrigerate for at least 1 hour before serving.

Turn each out of the mould onto a plate and, if necessary, run a knife around the edges to loosen them.

To make the sauce, mix together the first 3 ingredients until smooth and not too thick, so that when you pour the sauce over the panna cotta, it should slowly start to slide down its sides. Add a little nut milk or water to thin it down, if necessary.

Oat milk and cream can be substituted with soya/soy milk and cream with the same results. If you decide to make panna cotta out of homemade Nut Milk (page 16 – hazelnut is best for this recipe), do bear in mind that homemade nut milks are less dense in flavour and less fatty, so the panna cotta turns a bit more watery than if made with pre-bought milk. Also, homemade nut milks tend to separate slightly while this dessert is chilling in the fridge, so you end up with a translucent top and a more milk-coloured base. Still, it will be your own homemade panna cotta made from scratch! The sauce gives it extra nut flavour and sweetness, so don't omit it!

# fluffy cake with strawberry coulis

This is a lovely light vegan cake to serve at tea parties, topped with fruit coulis or jam, if fresh berries are out of season. Chestnut flour gives it a subtle nutty aroma, but substituting it with cocoa powder, carob powder or grain coffee powder works well, too.

## For the cake

30 g/¼ cup chestnut flour (or cocoa powder, carob powder or grain coffee powder)

zest and juice of 1 organic lemon

155 ml/⅔ cups soy/soya milk

140 g/1 cup millet flour

30 g/¼ cup wholemeal/whole wheat oat flour

½ teaspoon bicarbonate of soda/baking soda

½ teaspoon aluminium-free baking powder

¼ teaspoon bourbon vanilla powder

⅛ teaspoon sea salt

3 tablespoons sunflower oil

150 g/½ cup rice syrup

## For the strawberry coulis

320 g/2 cups fresh strawberries

2 tablespoons maple syrup

1 teaspoon lemon juice

pinch of sea salt

24-cm/ 9½-in. springform cake pan

Serves 6–8

If you're using chestnut flour that hasn't been pre-roasted, place it in a dry frying pan/skillet over a medium heat and stir until fragrant and golden. Set aside.

Add the lemon juice to the milk and let sit for 10 minutes. Meanwhile, sift the chestnut, millet and oat flour with the bicarbonate of soda/baking soda and baking powder and then add the vanilla and salt. Mix well with your hand or with a whisk.

Before you bake your cake, you can prepare the coulis by mixing all the ingredients and letting them sit for 30 minutes. Mash with a fork to get a juicy coulis with some texture. You can also blend it if you prefer a smooth sauce.

Preheat the oven to 180°C (350°F) Gas 4. Cover the bottom of the springform pan with parchment paper, attach the cake ring and cut away the excess paper. Oil the bottom and the sides of the pan. Add the oil and syrup to the milk and lemon mixture and mix well with a spatula. Make sure you don't mix too much, otherwise the cake might turn chewy. Now, pour the batter into your prepared cake pan and spread evenly. Bake for 18–20 minutes. Test if done by inserting a cocktail stick/toothpick into the middle of the cake; if it comes out clean, it's done.

Let the cake cool completely, and then cut with a bread knife into 6–8 equal slices. Spoon the coulis over the cake slices just before serving.

# the quickest & yummiest ice-cream

This type of ice-cream is very popular with raw foodies, but becomes an instant favourite with anybody who tries it. Even though many similar recipes are available on-line, I wanted to share with you my three favourite combinations made with the same base, i.e. fully ripe frozen bananas!

### In advance
3 ripe bananas

a plastic bag

### For berry ice-cream, add to the sliced bananas
160 g/1¼ cups frozen or fresh raspberries, sour-cherries, etc.

¼ teaspoon bourbon vanilla powder

2 tablespoons agave syrup

### For double cocoa ice-cream, add to the sliced bananas
2 tablespoons raw cocoa powder

2 tablespoons agave syrup

¼ teaspoon ground cinnamon

1 tablespoon raw cocoa nibs (mix in after blending)

### For cappuccino-hazelnut ice-cream, add to the sliced bananas
2 tablespoons grain coffee powder

1 teaspoon coffee extract

2 tablespoons maple syrup

¼ teaspoon bourbon vanilla powder

4 tablespoons dry-roasted hazelnuts, chopped (mix in after blending)

### All recipes serve 2

Peel the bananas and put them together in a plastic bag. Put the bag in the freezer and freeze them until they're completely hard. Take out of the freezer 10 minutes before using.

Slice the frozen bananas with a sharp knife. Place the banana slices and all other ingredients for that particular ice-cream in a high-speed blender. Blend on the high setting and use the tamper (a tool that comes with the blender, which is used to push the ingredients down into the blades) to accelerate the blending process.

You might be able to make these ice-creams in a food processor, too, but it will probably take longer and turn out on the softer side because of the longer blending time. Serve immediately!

# dark chocolate tart

*Combining dark chocolate with a slightly sour berry sauce is a delicious and healthy dessert. In conventional recipes, ganache is made from cream, but I use soft tofu instead and the result is a smooth and rich ganache.*

### For the crust

200 g/1½ cups unbleached plain/all-purpose flour

75 g/½ cup fine cornflour/cornstarch

1 teaspoon aluminum-free baking powder

¼ teaspoon sea salt

120 g/½ cup non-hydrogenated margarine, chilled

60 g/scant ¼ cup brown rice syrup or agave syrup

zest of 1 organic lemon

### For the ganache

600 g/20 oz. medium-soft tofu

400 g/14 oz. vegan dark/bittersweet chocolate (60–70% cocoa), in pieces

1 tablespoon lemon juice concentrate

zest of 2 organic lemons

brown rice syrup, or other sweetener, to taste (optional)

a little non-dairy milk or cream, if necessary

### For the sauce

300 g/2 cups blueberries, fresh or frozen

120 ml/½ cup water

170 g/½ cup rice syrup or heaping ¾ cup demerara/raw brown sugar

1 organic lemon, zest and juice

1 tablespoon kuzu or cornflour/cornstarch

28-cm/11 in.-springform cake pan or 28-cm/11-in tart pan

Serves 12

To make the crust, combine the flours, baking powder and salt in a food processor and use the pulse setting to mix. Add the margarine and pulse 6–8 times until the mixture resembles coarse meal, with pea-sized pieces of margarine. Add the syrup and lemon zest and pulse again a couple of times. If you pinch some of the crumbly dough and it holds together, it's ready. If the dough doesn't hold together, add a little water and pulse again. Be careful not to add too much water, as it will make the crust tough. Place the dough in a mound on a clean work surface. Work the dough just enough to form a ball – do not over-knead. Form a disc, wrap in clingfilm/plastic wrap and refrigerate for at least 3 hours, but it's best to leave it overnight. Let the dough sit at room temperature for 5–10 minutes before rolling.

Preheat the oven to 180°C (350°F) Gas 4. For the ganache, blanch the tofu in a pan for 10 minutes and then drain it. In a double boiler (see page 127 for instructions), melt the chocolate. Blend the tofu with the chocolate, lemon juice and zest in a blender until very smooth. If it's too bitter, blend in the syrup. If it's too thick, add non-dairy milk or cream while blending.

Take the dough out of the fridge and roll it between 2 sheets of parchment paper into a circle 31 cm/12¼ in. in diameter. With the help of a rolling pin, line the cake/tart pan with the dough. Trim the edges using a pastry wheel, if using a springform pan, or remove the excess dough by pressing it outwards with your fingers, if using a tart pan. Patch up any holes with leftover dough. Prick the base all over with a fork and bake for 8–10 minutes. Spoon the ganache over the crust and even it with a spatula. Return to the oven and bake until the edges turn lightly golden, around 15 minutes. Take it out of the oven and let cool.

For the sauce, combine the blueberries, water, syrup or sugar and lemon zest and juice in a saucepan over a medium heat. Bring to a slow boil, stirring occasionally. In a small bowl, mix the kuzu or cornflour/cornstarch with a little cold water. Stir this slowly into the sauce, without crushing the berries. Simmer for about 5 minutes or until reaching the desired thickness. While still warm, spoon over each slice of the pie just before serving.

# crêpes Dunjette

This is a healthier version of the famous Crêpes Suzette, and since they are egg-, sugar- and butter-free, I named them Crêpes Dunjette, after me! I use agave syrup and coconut oil, and the result is irresistible.

165 ml/¾ cup soya/soy milk

110 ml/½ cup water

¼ teaspoon aluminium-free bicarbonate of soda/baking soda

¼ teaspoon sea salt

130 g/1 cup unbleached plain/all-purpose flour or millet flour

coconut oil, for frying

### For the glaze

8 tablespoons agave syrup

zest and juice of 4 organic blood (or regular) oranges (see Note)

4 tablespoons extra virgin coconut oil, plus extra to finish

2–4 tablespoons rum (optional)

80 g/2¾ oz. dark/bittersweet vegan chocolate

Serves 4

In a mixing bowl, combine the soya/soy milk and water. Add the baking powder and salt. Slowly add the flour, whisking vigorously with a balloon whisk. The batter should be thicker than pancake batter made with eggs. Let it stand for at least 15 minutes.

Heat a frying pan/skillet and add a little coconut oil before pouring in the batter for each pancake. Pour a small ladleful of the batter into the pan and tilt the pan to spread the batter evenly over the surface. Once the edges start turning golden brown, flip the pancake over. The batter should make 8 medium-sized pancakes.

Heat half the agave syrup in a separate frying pan/skillet over a medium heat until slightly caramelized. Add the remaining agave syrup and the orange juice and zest and bring to a slow boil. Add the coconut oil. The glaze shouldn't be too thick.

Pour most of the glaze from the pan into a bowl. Place a pancake in the pan and fold over twice to coat it well in the glaze. Add more glaze for the second pancake and repeat until you use up all the pancakes. At the end, add little rum if you wish, for a richer aroma.

In a double boiler (see page 127 for instructions), melt the chocolate and stir in a few drops of coconut oil to make it glossy. Drizzle over the pancakes just before serving.

Note: If you've only been able to get non-organic oranges, you can release water-soluble pesticides from the rind by placing the oranges in a bowl and covering with warm water; add 2 teaspoons salt and 2 teaspoons aluminium-free bicarbonate of soda/baking soda and let stand for at least 10 minutes. Pat the oranges dry then grate the zest and squeeze the juice.

# coffee granita with whipped coconut cream

I'm not a coffee drinker, but I love the taste of coffee in cakes and desserts. Coffee substitutes are very similar in taste, but without the side effects, so this dessert can be served to kids as well. In case you don't have time to whip up coconut cream, you can serve this granita with pre-bought soya/soy or rice whipped cream, even though the taste of coconut takes this dessert to another level of yumminess!

## For the granita

230 ml/1 cup water

45 g/¼ cup demerara/raw brown sugar

3 tablespoons coffee substitute (Yannoh, Bianca or Orzo), plus extra to serve

1 tablespoon coffee extract

¼ teaspoon bourbon vanilla powder

## For the whipped coconut cream

400-ml/14-oz. can coconut milk (60% fat), chilled overnight

1 tablespoon demerara/raw brown sugar

shaved vegan dark/bittersweet chocolate, to serve

Serves 3–4

To make the granita, mix the water and sugar in a saucepan and bring to a boil. Whisk in the coffee substitute and let boil again. Remove from heat and add the coffee extract and vanilla. Let cool completely, pour into a shallow dish and put in the freezer for 15 minutes.

Whisk with a fork to distribute the frozen parts and break up the crystals. Freeze again until icy at the edge of pan and the overall texture is slushy, about 25 minutes. Whisk with a fork, put back in the freezer and whisk again after 20 minutes to distribute the frozen portions evenly. Cover and return to the freezer. When ready to serve, remove from the freezer and scrape the granita with a fork, forming icy flakes. You can make granita a couple of days ahead.

To make the whipped coconut cream, open the chilled coconut milk without shaking it, since it will separate and you only need the solid fatty part. Scrape this solid part out into a tall and narrow bowl; just be careful not to mix in any liquid from the bottom, since this will prevent the cream from whipping up properly. With a freestanding mixer (or an electric hand mixer), mix on high speed for 2–3 minutes until it starts getting thicker. Add the sugar and whip for another 3–5 minutes. Be patient! Sometimes the cream gets soft peaks, and sometimes it stays fluffy, depending how good you were in separating the solid part from the liquid. In any case, it is very tasty! If you want the cream to be snow-white, use icing/confectioners' sugar instead of demerara/raw brown sugar.

To serve, scoop the granita into parfait glasses, top with the whipped coconut cream and sprinkle with coffee substitute or shaved chocolate, as preferred. Serve immediately.

# crumble in a glass

Crumble is an excellent dessert, but the problem with the traditional baked crumble and fruit combination is that it has to be eaten freshly made, since the crumbly topping soaks up the fruit juice after a while and you're left with soggy leftovers. For this reason, I decided to make a recipe for a crumble that will always stay crispy, and that you can make in advance.

### For the crumble topping

50 g /½ cup walnut halves

130 g/1 cup unbleached plain/ all-purpose or millet flour

80 g/⅓ cup demerara/raw brown sugar

¼ teaspoon ground cinnamon

pinch of sea salt

90 g/scant ½ cup non-hydrogenated margarine, chilled

### For the fruit base

500–600 g/18–21 oz. fresh fruit, prepared weight (depending on the season, you can use mangoes, pears, apples, peaches, cherries or plums)

125 ml/½ cup water

6 tablespoons agave or maple syrup

¼ teaspoon bourbon vanilla powder or ground cinnamon

2 teaspoons lemon juice

Serves 4

Preheat the oven to 180°C (350°F) Gas 4. Spread the walnuts on a baking sheet (you can also toast more nuts than you actually need, to use them as a snack) and toast for 10 minutes. Take the nuts out of the oven, let them cool and then coarsely chop them. In a bowl, combine the flour, sugar, cinnamon and salt. Add the margarine and rub it into the dry ingredients until you get a fine crumbly consistency without big pieces of margarine left. Now add the chopped walnuts. Spread on a parchment paper-lined baking sheet and bake for 15–17 minutes, stirring it every 5 minutes to prevent uneven baking. Let cool and then store in a tightly closed jar.

Before serving the crumble, wash, peel, stone/pit and cut your fruit into wedges. In case the fruit is very ripe and soft (this is especially the case with mangoes, peaches, apricots and pears), just blend them into a purée in a food processor or blender withthe remaining ingredients. If the fruit is only fairly ripe or slightly under-ripe, put it in a saucepan and add the water (it should go 1 cm/⅓ in. up the side of the pot), syrup and the vanilla or cinnamon. Cover, bring to a boil, lower the heat to the absolute minimum and simmer for 10 minutes, or longer, if you want very soft fruit. Next, mix in the lemon juice.

Take a dessert glass and layer it generously with tablespoons of the fruit, then 3 tablespoons of the crumble topping. Repeat with 3 other glasses and they're ready to serve!

# index

# acknowledgments

I'd like to thank:
Everybody I mentioned in my previous cookbooks – the support I get from all the loving people around me is everlasting and keeps me safe and happy!

The new Ryland Peters & Small team members who worked hard to make this book as beautiful as it is!

No acknowledgment can pass without thanking the furry members of our family for being so soft and fluffy! Relaxing after a hard day's work in the kitchen could not be as effective and enjoyable without our two silly cats sleeping in our laps or following us on our afternoon walks to the woods!

And, I have to thank nature for providing us with its wonderful fruits, which inspire me to create new recipes that nurture our bodies and souls...